Contents

Acknowledgments

While I was a collector of Depression Glass long before I collected Christmas, I had not even thought of creating a book on the subject. However, upon the encouragement of Peter Schiffer and Doug Congdon-Martin I undertook this task.

In my college days Depression glass and its bright vivid colors attracted my interest. Even though collecting Christmas quickly became an obsession for me, I continued to pick up glass over the years. My wife Sharon and I share this common interest. In fact, it was her renewed interest in Manhattan, Tea Room, and Pyramid that further sparked our searches for Depression glass. But it soon became evident that our collection was not substantial enough to do a book of any magnitude.

Coming to our rescue were two very delightful and knowledgeable Depression glass enthusiasts and experts. Ray and Virginia Miller of Spring Green, Wisconsin, graciously allowed us and Doug Congdon-Martin to spend many, many hours in their wonderful antique shop photographing piece upon piece of glass.

The Millers graciously added many tidbits of information during and after these photography sessions. Ray and Virginia also greatly helped with the price guide in evaluating fair prices for these marvelous pieces of glass. It is the Millers' generosity and expertise that helped to mold this book. Sharon and I are very indebted to them for their friendship and graciousness extended to us.

There are no doubts that any Depression glass collectors who seek more information or who are searching for this wonderful glassware will find their visit to the Millers in Spring Green as one of their highlights in a collecting career. Even a phone conversation will reveal that vibrant and enthusiastic dedication these two individuals have to Depression glass and its collecting.

Interestingly enough, technology played a major role in this book as well. With the help of the Internet and collectors on line, we were able to better evaluate prices and develop a price guide more reflective of current times.

Even though countless individuals were of great assistance in compiling the information in this book, I wish to especially thank Harriet Glover, Sophie and Spike Brievogel, Mike Makurat, Brian Swanson, and Fred Studach.

But most of all, I wish to thank all of the Depression glass collectors, dealers, and individuals who appreciate the beauty of this very humble, yet elegant glass.

Virginia and Ray Miller

History of Depression Glass Era

Depression glass has seen waves of collecting in the decades since it was first produced. However, a great amount of interest has developed in the past few years. This book is intended as a primer for Depression glass collectors. There is such a vast amount of knowledge and different patterns that it would be impossible to cover them within the confines of these covers. However, you will gain some new and intriguing insights as you turn these pages. Whether you are a beginner or a veteran collector, some very exciting discoveries lie around the corner.

Once again, collectors are drawn to this era of American glass manufacturing by the thousands—an era in which we turned to machine-made glass in huge quantities. Perhaps this interest is fueled in part by our keen interest in technology and all its marvels. It is this interest that has sparked renewed enthusiasm in veteran collectors as well as in collectors who previously almost ignored this style of glassware. To better understand this glass, it helps to put it into historical perspective.

While many term the years 1930-1935 as the "Golden Age of Depression Glass," those were harsh years of reality for most Americans. With the stock market crash in 1929, hopes for a quick recovery quickly disappeared as economic conditions worsened throughout 1930 and 1931.

Millions of Americans lost their jobs and the election of Franklin Roosevelt and his subsequent introduction of the New Deal offered hope, but little immediate improvement was realized for the average American citizen. Thus many people question just how all this colored glass was produced.

Part of the answer lies in the Pittsburgh Glass Exhibit in 1925. Glassmakers from Ohio, Indiana, Pennsylvania, New Jersey, and West Virginia were there to display their new wares to the buyers who had come from throughout the United States for this event. There was much excitement since housewives were buying more glass than ever before. Glass manufacturers foresaw a time when glass would replace all china and pottery. Everyone was bragging about expansion and the development of new plants.

There were those who doubted all this. Some even questioned the production of machine-made tumblers rolling off assembly lines. They asked, "Will the people really buy it?"

These individuals felt that machinery could not possibly be built that would produce glass in such huge quantities. Despite the fact that crystal decorated glass was the clear majority represented at the 1925 exhibit, this was nonetheless the crucial year in deciding the color questions. Some companies had been sending out some short lines of ornamental glass in colors, in transparent shades, quite new to the American industry.

The colorful lines were quite successful. Among those who had come to this Exhibit were countless buyers. They were enthused about canary, blue, amber, green, and amethyst, and the new rosy pale pink shade was in the works for fall release. By the end of the Exhibit, few companies were thinking crystal as they left. They were now dreaming in color and wondering what else could be designed in these colors.

Production momentum was now in the manufacturers' favor. They had explored new technologies as early as 1925 and made the commitment to the machine production of colored glassware. Based on the prosperity of the late 1920s, much capital and energy had been spent on tanks, piping, molds, and other such automated equipment. Even though they faced the bleak reality of the 1930s, they had no choice but to move forward with what they had begun. How else were they going to survive?

These companies were perfecting the process of mold etching. Mold etching turned the traditional approach to glass decoration "inside out." In traditional etching acid was applied to the glassware by skilled artisans. Thus the patterns appeared intaglio, that is, cut into the surface of the glass. This was a very time consuming method and extremely expensive; only the finer glass houses used it. Such glassware is termed elegant glass of this Depression era.

Faced with their very survival, companies needed to cut production costs. Thus the patterns represented in this book were manufactured by using acid to cut the pattern into a mold, rather than on the glass itself. When molten glass was piped into these molds, the result was a surface design in relief, the opposite of acid etching. However, the appearance was quite similar. By reducing the amount of skilled human workmanship the companies could produce this glass so much more inexpensively.

The glass mixture itself was usually of the cheapest quality, consisting mostly of silica, soda ash, and lime. With the lower quality of glass, the mold-etch decorating technique served a second purpose of hiding the inevitable flaws such as bubbles and cloudiness. *Madrid* is a good example of this. The festoons and feathered scrolls combined with the bold, dominant center diamond motif to create a pattern that pleases the eye, but also distracts it from a too-close examination of the few surface areas that were left blank. Bubbles and other flaws in the glass itself are thus hidden from the casual eye.

But then if these glass companies produced this glass to survive, basic questions come to mind. How was it marketed and sold in a time of such harsh, economic realities? American businesses were determined to survive these times of little money. To do this, one scheme they developed was the marketing strategy of the purchase premium used to entice customers to spend their scarce, hard-earned dollars. It worked. People bought a specific brand of oatmeal or soap just to obtain the piece of useful, colorful glass packed directly in the box or container.

Many Americans remember from childhood the anticipation when the new box of oatmeal was opened. Their curiosity was piqued. What "goodie" had the manufacturer packed into the box? Quaker Oats Company of Chicago, Illinois, packed premiums into their boxes of oatmeal for many years. Forest Green consisting of tumblers, juice, glasses, sherbets, dessert dishes, and plates were packed into their boxes for quite some time. "Blue Bubble" was a popular premium, thus its abundance today. In the 1930s *Mothers Oats* was a prime source of dishes and glassware, with "Miss America" as one of its premiums.

Seed packets (very popular with Americans who planted their own gardens for survival) and even magazine subscriptions were promoted by giving Depression glass as a premium. Entire sets could be amassed though coupon programs. Just by viewing 1930s magazine advertisements, one can easily locate ads for glassware offered as premiums for the purchase of flour, furniture, and even theater tickets. This interdependent relationship benefited both the American businesses as well as glass companies producing the glass itself.

This effort to continually lure buyers and collectors meant that countless patterns in a variety of colors were produced. There was something for everyone. Many patterns were produced in full dinner services with numerous accessory pieces. Some premiums were merely smaller sized luncheon sets or bridge sets.

While the majority of Depression glass was produced by the mold-etched method, other creative forms of glass design were pursued. Such evidence lies in Sierra, created by Jeannette Glass Company in 1931. It was a most daring design, but the sharp edges chipped far too easily. Thus it quickly came to the end of its production, with pieces subsequently being very rare today.

Brief Histories of Major Depression Glass Manufacturers

While many of us enjoy Depression glass for what it is, there is always the inevitable question, "Who produced all this glass?" The questions are easily answered by "So many different glass companies…some of, which are still unknown today." But some of the major producers of Depression glass should be recognized by collectors today for their fabulous contributions to this history. What follows is a compilation of those major companies with a brief history of each so those collectors might have a truer sense of appreciation of what they collect.

Cambridge Glass Company of Cambridge, Ohio

Cambridge had its origins in the National Glass Company. Out of this beginning, this company went on to become a major provider of glass for Americans. The young (built in 1901) Cambridge Company under private management began turning heads in less than a decade of its existence.

There is no doubt that this factory was a source and an inspiration for the colored glass trend. Excellent design, workmanship, and glass quality ranked Cambridge products at the top of the market. In the 1920s, an effective publicity campaign brought the Cambridge trademark—and the notion of color—before the public and linked this company trademark with ideas of elegance and prosperity. A result of their campaign, an ever-increasing demand for their products bought about factory expansion. After the company's closing in 1958, the molds went to the Imperial Glass Company, and some are still in use today in crystal and new colors.

Federal Glass Company of Columbus, Ohio

Federal Glass Company, founded in 1900, was a division of Federal Paper Board Company, of Columbus, Ohio. Beginning as a hand operation, making pressed crystal wares, plain or with needle etchings, Federal soon became attuned to the times. They quickly sensed the changes in consumer demands. Much early effort was channeled in developing methods which could produce huge amounts of glass automatically for a country now interested in economical tableware.

This switch to automation was a key to their early success. By the 1920s, Federal had become one of the largest suppliers of machine-made tumblers and jugs. By the 1930s, it had become one of the leaders in making the machine-pressed, mold-etched dinnerware in colors.

Many of the major patterns collected can be attributed to Federal. Such patterns as "Parrot," "Mayfair," and "Sharon" are among the most recognized. In addition, they produced "Colonial Fluted," "Columbia," "Diana," and "Georgian."

Interesting bits of knowledge include the fact that "Diana" was named for the daughter of G.H. Kuse of Indiana Glass Company. Some of the original workers remember spraying the amber carnival color on "Normandie." In the 1920s, Federal began utilizing green tanks of glass. Its first mold-etched pattern, "Georgian," was released in 1931.

In 1934, the "chipped-mold" method was employed to manufacture "Mayfair," "Sharon," and "Rosemary." In the latter part of the 1930s, Federal employed still another method for manufacturing glass, the "paste-mold method."

According to company spokesmen, sets were sold in a large volume throughout the year and became extremely popular during the Jewish Passover, and later in the year for summer cottage use. Cups retailed for five cents each.

The firm continued to expand tremendously. By the 1940s it had expanded into the food service industry. In 1958, Federal became a division of the Federal Paper Board Company.

On January 31, 1979, Federal ceased manufacturing.

Fenton Glass Company of Williamstown, West Virginia

Fenton was started in 1907, developing and producing Carnival glass. The firm's letterhead soon stated, "The Fenton Art Glass Company…Originators of Iridescent Ware." Founded by Frank L. Fenton and his brother John in Martins Ferry, Ohio, the company was off to a great start.

John Fenton's enthusiasm was well-documented. His personal appeals and flare for promotion was the ideal counterpart to Frank's business-like industry. For about two years the Fenton brothers decorated glass in an abandoned factory they had rented. Among the first to notice their success were the glass manufacturers who supplied the blanks for their decorating.

While riding a Wheeling streetcar one summer evening, John overheard passengers lamenting the bad luck of a Williamstown businessman who had lost his shirt in the Stock Market Crash. A few days later, John was in Williamstown acquiring real estate. Ground was broken for the new plant on October 7, 1906.

While carnival glass was its first effort, they soon turned their attention to highly textured pressed bowls, nut dishes, vases, and novelties.

The 1920s saw the Fenton line improve, both in quality and in design. The Stock Market Crash turned them to producing mixing bowls, juice extractors, liquefier bowls, and any other items that the sales force thought would sell. With such production lines, they were able to survive these very bad years.

Fenton Glass Company continued to be a leader in the glass production industry through the next decades, even a post-war recession for the handmade glass industry came and passed after World War II.

Hazel Atlas Company of Clarksville, West Virginia

Hazel Atlas Glass Company had its origins in 1885 at Wellsburg, West Virginia. Founded by C.N. Brady and Charles H. Tallman, it was formed to produce opal glass liners for Mason zinc caps. Why is "Hazel" part of its name? The name was chosen at random to name the company following a practice in the steel and iron industry of christening new furnaces with a feminine name. "Hazel" was not used for this new business as of March 1886. The company moved to Washington, Pennsylvania, where Hazel No. 1 plant produced its very first glass on January 10, 1887. In 1902, Hazel Glass Company and Atlas Glass and Metal Company became one Hazel-Atlas Glass Company and set up main offices at Wheeling, West Virginia.

The two Washington factories continued to make containers and new facilities were developed to break into other glass markets. By the time automation dawned upon the industry, most operations were geared to assembly-line production, and the companies thus enjoyed a great lead in this field. The Clarksburg, West Virginia plant specialized in pressed tablewares, pouring thousands upon thousands of pieces into the market. Two other factories in Zanesville, Ohio made thin-blown tumblers, containers, and other blown ware. Additional plants at Wheeling and Washington manufactured tableware as well as other kinds of containers.

The company expanded into nine widely distributed plants and continued in operation until it was sold to Brockway Glass Company, and Continental Can Company,

Clarksburg, West Virginia, in 1956. Brockway Glass Company bought it out in 1964, and then continued the factory.

Hazel Atlas is known for many of the tableware services and kitchenware of great abundance. So many tumblers were produced that this plant became known as the "World's Famous and Biggest Tumbler Factory" in America. They did not add color into their lines until 1929, but the green tumblers and mixing bowls released that year, took immediate hold. The next season they produced pink and topaz colors. Black glass was also being manufactured during this time.

In 1933, Killarney green, Sunset pink, and topaz were advertised for sale. Ritz blue appeared in 1936. They also attempted to produce red, but gradually produced Burgundy, a dark amethyst, instead. This was due to the extreme difficulty of producing a true red color.

Countless sets of green mixing bowls and dinnerware in opaque white glass are highly valued by collectors today. In an opaque color advertised as "Platonite," many tableware sets were released in the 1930s. The earliest "Platonite" was opalescent around the edges; later, it became fully opaque. One of their most recognizable patterns is "Royal Lace," a very decorative pattern in which the center of the plate is a cross of lacy scrolls, leaves, and flowers surrounded by a drape design.

Hocking Glass Company of Lancaster, Ohio

Isaac J. Collins, a native of Salisbury, Maryland, moved to Lancaster to head the decorating department of a small company called the Ohio Flint Glass Company. In 1905, the company went into receivership, and Collins, along with six friends succeeded in raising enough money. He called his company, Hocking Glass Company, named for the Hocking River near the plant. In 1924, the company suffered a tragic fire, reducing the plant to five acres of ashes and rubble. I. J. Collins and his associates were not to be discouraged.

Plans were soon devised to build a plant on top of the ashes of the old factory. Six months later, Plant 1 was in production—the company's first manufacturing facility specifically designed for the production of glassware. In 1924, Hocking also acquired controlling interest in what was then known as Lancaster Glass Company, later called Plant 2, and the Standard Glass Manufacturing Company with plants in Bremen, Ohio and Canal Winchester, Ohio.

During the mid-1920s, Hocking revolutionized tableware production with a machine that pressed glass automatically, boosting production, from one item a minute to 20, then to 35. It was reported that one Chicago store had sold 10,000 nineteen-piece sets of "Cameo" at one dollar a set, in only three days of a special sale. In one month alone, 25 carloads of these same water sets were sold.

Their color history is somewhat interesting to note. Green, blue, amber, and canary were marketed in occasional pieces in the mid-1920s. In 1926, Rose (first name for pink color) was seen for the first time. In 1928, topaz appeared; the blue of "Mayfair" premiered in 1930, and opaque white known as "Vitrock" was introduced in 1932.

The 1929 stock market crash, which put many companies out of business, merely sent Hocking's engineers back to the drawing board. They developed a 15-mold machine that made 90 pieces of glassware per minute. Now the company could sell tumblers, "two for a nickel" much less than half their former price. Despite the economic difficulties of the period, Hocking took a gigantic step in 1931, which made it much more than a glass table company. It entered the glass container business.

Hocking was formed in 1937 as a result of the merger of the Anchor Cap and Closure Corporation and its subsidiaries and the Hocking Glass Company. By this time, total employment had reached 6,000 and the company produced a wide range of glass tableware, glass containers, closures, and sealing machinery.

By far Hocking Glass was the largest producer of Depression tableware. Supplying glass for many catalog stores and large chain stores, they gained a reputation for producing some extremely beautiful patterns. Ice tubs, steak plates, and reamers are among the variety of glass utilitarian pieces produced over the years. Among their most recognizable patterns are "Bubble," "Hobnail," and "Miss America."

Hocking took over the Lancaster Glass Company, Standard Glass Company, and Monongah Glass Company. After the various mergers, Anchor Hocking Glass Corporation continued to expand its ideas and interests. In 1969, the company name was modified to Anchor Hocking Corporation to allow its more diversified status.

Imperial Glass Company of Bellaire, Ohio

Organized in 1901, Imperial Glass Company produced its first glass at the Bellaire, Ohio plant in 1904. Early products were hotel tumblers, pressed table items for five-and-dimes, and jelly glasses, but soon this company made its own distinctive mark. Their big splash was color and special color effects. Iridescent glass, produced from 1910-1920, was a precursor of depression glass, and is our Carnival glass today. "Imperial Jewels," started in 1916, is known today as stretch glass. And the "Free Hand Ware," made from 1923-1928 without any molds of any kind, is collected today as art glass.

In the 1920s an "imitation cut glass" known as "Nu-Cut" in crystal and transparent colors was offered. Complete lines of tableware were sold. With etchings, gold trims, and decorations; they became extremely popular. Luncheon sets were extremely popular at the time of the Depression, and this company produced thousands of them. However, the competition from machine-made glass houses during these lean years proved too much. They went out of business in 1932, but soon resurfaced as the Imperial Glass Corporation. The new management resumed production of the pressed color lines, and added some popular new patterns. They were anticipating a return to crystal, and this idea helped to spark its earlier prosperity in the market.

Their principal Depression-era colors included pink, green, and amber, which were on the scene by the mid 1920s. Golden green (known as Vaseline) was advertised early, but did not enjoy much popularity. Blue arrived in 1926 and blue-green in 1927. In 1929, a small assortment was offered in orchid, green, or ivory glass embellished with floral decals. In 1931, topaz and ruby were advertised; about this time Ritz blue and black were developed. Black was especially popular in the 1930s.

In 1940 Imperial acquired Central Glass Works of Wheeling, and, in 1958, they acquired molds of both Cambridge Glass and A.H. Heisey Company. Imperial was sold to Lenox, Inc. in 1973. Lenox-Imperial Glass was purchased in May of 1981 by Arthur Lorch. Attractive lines of largely hand-pressed gifts and housewares were the mainstays of the decade.

Arthur Lorch Imperial Glass was purchased by Robert Stahl in September, 1982. Mr. Stahl started to mark all the glass with a completely new trademark. In 1984 Mr. Stahl declared bankruptcy. The Imperial Glass Factory closed its door on April 11, 1985.

Indiana Glass Company of Dunkirk, Indiana

Currently known to collectors as Indiana Glass Company, it was founded in the 1890s as the Ohio Flint Glass Company. Later, it became the National Glass Company, which was taken over by the Beatty-Brady Glass Company in the early 1900s. The Indiana Glass Company was founded in 1907.

In 1929, Indiana had been making pressed patterns and hand-molded "Sandwich" in crystal. It then began to experiment with using pink and green as alternative colors for their products. These early pressed lines were of heavy and serviceable glass. They subsequently began to use the "mold-etch process" to etch delicate patterns on glassware.

With the advent of assembly-line production, Indiana Glass Company designed its glass production around machines. Thus much patterned ware by Indiana appeared on the market in the late 1920s.

"Tea Room" is probably the most recognized of the patterns produced. "Pyramid" is also one of those Depression patterns which is quickly purchased by Art Deco collectors. It should be noted that the company identified many of its patterns by number rather than name, although many patterns acquired names.

Indiana's colors were the classic ones of the Depression era. Amber and green had their beginnings in 1925. Rose appeared in 1926; topaz in 1930. Yet with the exception of amber, these colors enjoyed a short-lived popularity, passing out of production by the mid 1930s.

Jeannette Glass Company, Jeannette, Pennsylvania

Jeannette Glass Company was incorporated in 1889. By 1920, the company's early production in hand-made and blown glasswares shifted to fill the increased demand for vault lights and automobile light lenses.

As early as 1924, Jeannette was described by the trade as "one of the most complete automatic factories in the country." In 1927, the company announced the cessation of all hand operations in favor of machine ones. A few pieces of colored glass were being pressed in 1925. In 1928, the first complete tableware lines in color were marketed.

In 1929, the company had been producing crystal "Iris" and "Intaglio," as well as plain pitchers and tumblers in pink "Cubist."

Then, in 1930, Jeannette became the first in the field to produce a complete line of molded glass tableware simultaneously in three different colors—pink, green, and crystal—using automatic machinery. These first patterns included "Floral" and "Cherry Blossom." Jeannette Glass Company often repeated the styles of its sandwich trays, candlesticks, and handled bowls from pattern to pattern. It did create cookie jars with its tableware sets, and it was the only company to produce cone-shaped pitchers and child's sets in Depression glass. It was a major manufacturer, often advertising some items to be "sold by carload only."

During World War II the company produced glass food containers and glass caps. Early American lamp parts and soda fountain glassware were sold in huge quantities.

In 1961, Jeannette purchased the McKee glass factory and moved its production facilities and offices to the larger plant.

Jeannette's designs were modern and typical of the decorative art style of the period in which they were made. Counted among their patterns were "Adam," "Cherry Blossom," "Doric," and "Floral."

Iridescent glass was made from the early 1920s on. Apple green was introduced in 1925. A 27-piece bridge set in topaz was also offered in 1925. In 1926, amber appeared as well as green. In 1927, pink made its appearance. At this time green and pink were the two primary colors produced by Jeannette. Jadite appeared in 1932, and Deflite in 1936. Ultamarine was very popular in 1937 and 1938, and continued to be quite successful up to 1949, when it was discontinued.

Lancaster Glass Company, Lancaster, Ohio

Before Lancaster became a subsidiary of Hocking Glass Company, it existed in Ohio. First started in 1908 by the individual who had been the first president of the Fostoria Glass Company, it quickly thrived and grew. In 1924, it came under the control of Hocking. At that time Lancaster was producing cut and decorated tableware, kitchenware, and occasional pieces. It continued along these same lines with the Lancaster trademark until 1937.

Many blanks were distributed to Standard Glass Company for cutting and etching. Lancaster's colors in the 1920s included green, blue, and canary which was recorded in 1925. Pink was added in 1926, topaz in 1930, and pale blue and black in 1931. Frequently Lancaster applied gold decorations to their pieces.

Macbeth Glass Company, Charlerol, Pennsylvania

Now part of Corning Glass Work, Charlerol, Pennsylvania, Macbeth-Evans Glass company produced "American Sweetheart" and "Dogwood."

Macbeth (first producers of optical glass in the United States) and Evans (largest lamp chimney manufacturers in the world) merged in 1899. They combined so that they could build a new company around a just patented invention, the glass blowing machine. This early mechanization was a first step on the way to a new recognition in the glass blowing industry. In two decades, Macbeth had become one of the largest suppliers of glass for industry, science, and illumination.

For many years Macbeth had been searching for other markets. In the mid-1920s, they introduced water sets and tumblers. Prior to 1929, Macbeth had been producing crystal glassware, primarily by hand. But machine methods were arriving on the scene and Macbeth commenced making colored tableware, mostly in pink. Manufactured in crystal and colors; the first complete mold-etched tableware line was created in 1930. An outstanding success, other lines followed and Macbeth became famous in the manufacturing of machine-made color glass.

Macbeth-Evans merged with Corning in the early part of 1937. The firm continued with the trademark Macbeth-Evans into the 1940s.

Macbeth just didn't produce as much green as other companies, and rarely used yellow. Ruby Red and Ritz Blue hues were introduced in the mid-1930s in "American Sweetheart," both very desirable colors to collectors today. In addition, Macbeth produced "Roly Poly" tumblers, cocktail shakers, and ice tubs in these two colors as well.

White translucent Monax dates back prior to the 1920s when it was developed as the ideal glass for illumination. Most street lamps in every American city and town as well as school classrooms were illuminated by Monax globes. In the 1930s, Macbeth used some of their favorite creations in the their tableware lines, thus we were introduced to Cremax, Ivrene, and Denax.

McKee Glass Company, Jeannette, Pennsylvania

McKee Glass Company actually evolved from a family of glassmakers active in the Pittsburgh area since 1834, when the firm of McKee, Salisbury, and Company began manufacturing bottles and window glass. Two McKee companies operated simultaneously for over 36 years: S. McKee and Company (window glass and bottles) and McKee and

Brothers (tableware). Both companies were very active in the glass manufacturing business.

In 1888 the factory moved from Pittsburgh to a tiny Pennsylvania community thereafter known as Jeannette named for the wife of McKee's founder. McKee and Brothers merged with National Glass Company in 1898 and withdrew in 1900, to become McKee Glass Company.

The firm was reorganized in 1903 and called the McKee Glass Company. McKee Glass Company was purchased in 1951 by Thatcher Glass Manufacturing Company, and subsequently sold to Jeannette Glass Company in 1961.

Most of McKee's glass products were manufactured by hand with automatic methods introduced in the 1940s. Their products were generally marketed at the moderate price levels. Much kitchenware was a mainstay of the company, primarily the Glasbake line, first marketed in the period before World War I.

Colorful opaque glass was made from 1930 to 1940, and there is a reason behind this. McKee was hit hard by the Stock Market Crash and its production sharply curtailed. But the unique opaques including the Sunkist reamers were so popular with the public that the company was boosted from its low economic status.

In 1923, Jade Yellow, "Jap" blue, and amethyst were often times satin-finished or combined with black bases. Blue, amber, canary, and green were introduced in the latter part of 1923. Sky blue and Grass green appeared in 1925; rose pink in 1926; ruby and orchid in 1927; and Jade, Ritz blue, black, in 1930.

Paden City Glass Manufacturing Company, Paden City, West Virginia

Paden City Glass Manufacturing Company started in 1916. Located in Paden City, West Virginia, they made mostly pressed tableware at first. Much restaurant and hotel glass was made for a time. Paden City came into prominence in the 1920s when it began using color. Wine sets were offered in two dozen different color combinations. In addition to extremely large assortments of occasional pieces, several lines of colored dinnerware were made as well.

Paden City soon began to be recognized for its very high quality glass. In 1949, they underwent a redesign by new management, which included automation. Unfortunately, this new direction was not beneficial to the company, and it closed in 1951.

Black glass appeared in 1923 along with its crystal. Green, Mulberry, blue, and amber were advertised in 1924. Pink appeared in 1925. Black continued through the entire 1930s. Forest green and Ceylon blue were advertised in 1936. In 1936 Paden City advertised its dark blue, which collectors refer to as Cobalt blue. It was one of the very few companies to promote this color.

L.E. Smith, Mt. Pleasant, Pennsylvania

This Company has its origins in Lewis E. Smith who was an occupational drifter, out of work more than in it. Smith was a gourmet cook, however, and while working as a chef in Mt. Pleasant in 1907, he devised his own special recipe for mustard. Smith decided to market his mustard. "Smith's German Mustard" was produced and canned all at one location. Before long sherbet glasses, salt and pepper shakers, and other small items were added to the glassware line.

In the spring of 1913, two fires caused major damage to the facilities. Mount Pleasant residents, not waiting to lose the industry because of inadequate fire insurance, raised the money to install a water supply and two fire hydrants for the factory.

After rebuilding, the plant produced a new line of goods. Vault lights (commonly known as glass blocks or bricks) were a major item.

Nearby the restaurant where he worked, there was an abandoned glass factory. So Smith decided to cut out the middleman and manufacture his own containers for the mustard. Once he started, Smith became completely absorbed in the concepts of glass making. Smith became quite successful, but suddenly he left this occupation and once again was out of work.

Interesting enough, he is credited for inventing the glass top for percolators, the modern-style juice reamer, the first glass mixing bowl, and other kitchen wares—no doubt inspired by his job as a chef in Mt. Pleasant. Smith also developed and produced the first automotive headlights for Ford Motor Company. Subsequent owners never changed the name because "it was always such an easy name to spell."

In the 1910s, Smith Glass Company was one of the largest factories in the country producing hand-made glass. Carnival glass was one of their specialties in the 1910s.

Black glass items were very prolific in the 1920s and 1930s. It can be safely said that Smith was the largest manufacturer of black glass during this period. Green, amber, canary, amethyst, and blue all appeared in 1926 with pink appearing in 1927.

Westmoreland Company, Grapeville, Pennsylvania

The Westmoreland Specialty Company was founded in October, 1889. Its site is near the large supplies of natural gas needed in the production of glass. Westmoreland Glass was under the management of the Brainard family for many generations and has occupied the same factory site since its beginnings in 1889.

Specialty Glass was incorporated in 1888 and started erecting buildings in July 1889. However it ran out of funds in October, 1889. At this point, Charles H. and George R. West invested $40,000 to finance the operation of Specialty Glass. The West brothers were formerly dry goods merchants in East Liberty, Pennsylvania.

After the West brothers purchased the business in 1889, the name was changed to Westmoreland Specialty Company.

While glass was its primary product, the company also processed baking powder, vinegar, mustard, and other condiments to fill their glass containers. During World War I glass items filled with candy were produced, and sold via dime stores and newsstands across America. Attracting so much attention that the public began making some very outlandish and strange requests for "specialties," it decided to drop "Specialty" from its name. On March 24, 1924, the board of directors of Westmoreland Specialty applied to change its name to Westmoreland Glass Company. The application was officially approved on February 10, 1925.

Concentrating thus on glassware, decorations and reproductions then became the specialty. In the early 1920s, Westmoreland doubled its capacity and became the largest decorating facility known. Such patterns as "Hobnail" and "Dolphins" were recreated and a career of milk glass production commenced.

By 1923, Westmoreland created fired-on solid colors, fancy decorations, and black and white stained glass. Amber appeared in 1924; green and blue appeared in 1925; and rose followed in 1926. Crystal and black glass combinations were sold in 1929. Crystal and topaz along with decorations on black and topaz were advertised for 1930. Belgian blue, a very deep blue color appeared in 1931. By 1935, Westmoreland had returned to a largely crystal production.

In 1980, J.H. Brainard started searching for a buyer for Westmoreland. David Grossman, a St. Louis, Missouri based distributor, purchased Westmoreland in March, 1981. Even though Grossman tried new lines and colors, the end came in 1984 when production ceased after the close of business on January 8, 1984. The items in stock were sold and auctions soon started to sell the equipment and glass.

About the values in this book:

The values here are here and now. They are derived from a variety of sources including the Internet, antique publications listing glass for sale, shop prices from around the country, antique show and sale prices, and estate sale prices.

Collectors need to be aware that prices do vary. However, the prices in this book reflect as accurately as possible the current market trends in the sale and purchasing of this glassware.

This is a guide, and a guide only. Of course, people will pay many times the book price for an item, especially if they know it is rare or if it is the last piece they need for a complete set. In addition, the moment when a buyer and seller meet often contains emotion. Therefore, collectors should realize that many factors come into play.

The Glassware

Adam

9" square dinner plate

Jeannette Glass Company, 1932-34
Colors: pink, green, delphite blue, topaz, yellow, crystal

Characterized by a leafy, feathery design, this glassware was extremely popular in its very short production history. With plates, saucers, and other pieces in the characteristic square design, it stands apart from most round shaped depression ware. In fact, many collectors find its variations its main collecting interest. Most often found in pink, it was also produced in green. Green is decidedly more expensive. As a result, pink is the favored color of most collectors. Never reissued, this pattern is extremely collectible since a full table service is possible.

Variations to look for are the pitchers found with both the round and the square bases; butter dishes whose lids are found with the Adam pattern or a combination of the Adam with the Sierra pattern on the lids. The Sierra design is found on the outside and the Adam design is found on the inside. Collectors should be aware that the candy and sugar lids are identical.

Reproduction Note: A.A. Importing Co. has manufactured Butter dish in Pink, Inc. It is 6-inches across. The new piece has a decidedly "washed-out pink color.

Sherbet, grill plate, salad plate, berry bowls with master berry bowl

Dinner plate, sherbet, and large berry bowl

ADAM

	Pink	Green		Pink	Green
Ash tray, 4-1/2"	$35	$30	Pitcher, 32 oz. round base	$70	
Bowl, 4-3/4" dessert	$20	$20	Plate, 6" sherbet	$9	$10
Bowl, 5-3/4" cereal	$55	$55	Plate, 7-3/4" square salad	$25	$25
Bowl, 7-3/4"	$35	$35	Plate, 9" square dinner	$35	$30
Bowl, 9", no cover	$50	$50	Plate, 9" grill	$30	$30
Bowl, cover, 9"	$40	$60	Platter, 11-3/4"	$33	$36
Bowl, 9" covered	$95	$100	Relish dish, 8" divided	$20	$25
Bowl, 10" oval	$35	$38	Salt & pepper, 4" ftd.	$100	$125
Butter dish & cover	$100	$400	Saucer, 6" square	$10	$10
Cake plate, 10" ftd.	$25	$28	Sherbet, 3"	$30	$35
Candlesticks, 4" pr.	$100	$120	Sugar	$20	$20
Candy jar & cover, 2-1/2"	$110	$130	Sugar/candy cover	$25	$40
Coaster, 3-1/4"	$25	$25	Tumbler, 4-1/2"	$30	$28
Creamer	$25	$25	Tumbler, 5-1/2" iced tea	$65	$65
Cup	$25	$24	Vase, 7-1/2"	$400	$70
Pitcher, 8", 32 oz.	$50	$55			

9¾" dinner plate

MacBeth-Evans Glass Company, 1930-36
Colors: pink, monax, red, blue, crystal, smoke

Very lacy and intricate, this pattern was heralded as a "decided favorite in the feminine eye" in an early company catalog advertising this pattern for sale. Pink is the most common color followed by monax. Macbeth was the only company to make *American Sweetheart*, and after 1936, it was never reissued.

American Sweetheart appeals to every beginning collector. Its intricate design is absolutely elegant when arranged on a table or in a china cabinet. Its appeal also lies in the fact that most pieces are abundant, thus somewhat easy to collect. However, prices are quite high for the more difficult-to-locate pieces.

Another characteristic of this pattern is the thin delicate glass, especially in the tumblers and water pitcher. The shakers and the pitchers are the most difficult to find in this pattern. It appears that pitcher and tumblers were made in pink only. Interesting enough,

Dinner, salad, bread and butter plate, cup, saucer, tumbler

this one of the few patterns that contains a sherbet with no stem or base. The crystal sherbets were meant to fit into a metal base.

The patterns are found both on the front and reverse sides, and sometimes in a combination of sides. Often on the monax pieces, the center portion of the design is omitted altogether. A gold-rimmed Monax piece indicates a manufacturing date of 1935 or later. That is the year when Macbeth added the gold rim.

Cream soup, two styles of sherbets, and cereal bowl

Salver, oval bowl, oval platter, and large round berry bowl

Very rare 8", 80oz. Pitcher

Very difficult to find salt and pepper shakers

9 ¾" monax dinner plate

Very hard to find 15 ½" salver in red

Creamer and sugar

Round berry bowl, creamer, sugar, and salver

10 ¼" dinner plate,
salad plate, cup, saucer,
cereal bowl, and sherbet

AMERICAN SWEETHEART

	Pink	Monax		Pink	Monax
Bowl, 3-3/4" flat berry	$75		Plate, 15-1/2" server		$250
Bowl, 4-1/2" cream soup	$85	$125	Platter, 13" oval	$60	$70
Bowl, 6" cereal	$20	$18	Pitcher, 7-1/2", 60 oz.	$900	
Bowl, 9" round berry	$60	$75	Pitcher, 8", 80 oz.	$700	
Bowl, 9-1/2" flat soup	$90	$100	Salt and pepper, ftd.	$600	$500
Bowl, 11" oval vegetable	$75	$80	Saucer	$4	$2
Bowl, 18" console		$450	Sherbet, 3-3/4" ftd.	$25	
Creamer, ftd.	$13	$10	Sherbet, 4-1/4" ftd.	$20	$22
Cup	$20	$12	Sherbet in metal holder (crystal only)	$8	
Plate, 6"	$6	$7	Sugar, open, ftd.	$15	$8
Plate, 8" salad	$11	$9	Sugar lid		$425
Plate, 9" luncheon		$12	Tid-bit, 2 tier, 8" & 12"	$60	$60
Plate, 9-3/4" dinner	$50	$30	Tid-bit, 3 tier, 8", 12" & 15-1/2"		$310
Plate, 10-1/4" dinner		$25	Tumbler, 3-1/2", 5 oz.	$100	
Plate, 11" chop plate		$18	Tumbler, 4-1/4", 9 oz.	$100	
Plate, 12" salver	$25	$20	Tumbler, 4-3/4", 10 oz.	$120	

Sherbets illustrating the paneled and diamond pattern of *Aunt Polly*

U.S. Glass Company, late 1920s
Colors: green, blue, and iridescent

Blue is the most prevalent and highest priced in this pattern. It was first advertised in green in a Sears Roebuck catalog. The entire set of 20 pieces retailed for $2.50. Rarest and most difficult to find are the oval bowls, sugars with cover, and salt and pepper shakers.

AUNT POLLY

	Green, Iridescent	Blue		Green, Iridescent	Blue
Bowl, 4-3/4" berry	$10	$20	Pitcher, 8", 48 oz.		$195
Bowl, 4-3/4", 2" high	$15		Plate, 6" sherbet	$8	$15
Bowl, 5-1/2" one handle	$15	$25	Plate, 8" luncheon		$20
Bowl, 7-1/4" oval, handled pickle	$15	$40	Salt and pepper		$285
Bowl, 7-7/8" large berry	$25	$50	Sherbet	$15	$20
Bowl, 8-3/8" oval	$45	$110	Sugar	$25	$30
Butter dish and cover	$250	$230	Sugar cover	$75	$180
Candy, cover, 2-handled	$75		Tumbler, 3-5/8", 8 oz.		$30
Candy, ftd., 2-handled	$30	$50	Vase, 6-1/2" ftd.	$40	$60
Creamer	$30	$60			

Creamer, sugar bowl, and 6 ½" round bowl in Vaseline color

Imperial Glass Company, 1927-1930s
Colors: amber, iridescent, blue, opalescent, crystal, pink, green, vaseline

This pattern has quite a good, heavy quality feel to it. Often associated with pattern glass or opalescent glass, it was manufactured in this era and was inexpensively priced qualifying it as Depression glass.

Especially desirable are the blue and Vaseline colors, which are generally more high priced than the other colors. Often times, this pattern goes undetected and is missed by beginning collectors. However, in the past few years, *Beaded Block* is finding unbelievable interest among collectors. As a result, prices are steadily rising.

Round plates are very difficult to locate; it seems that most of them were made into bowls by rolling the edges of the plate to create a bowl. As a result, plates, bowls, and many other pieces created are difficult to measure. The most difficult to locate in this pattern seem to be the pitcher and covered candy jar.

Reproduction Note: Items are being manufactured today, but they are mold embossed with a small "IG." This trademark was added in February, 1951.

BEADED BLOCK

	Crystal, Pink, Green, Amber	Other Colors		Crystal, Pink, Green, Amber	Other Colors
Bowl, 4-7/8"-5" 2-handled jelly	$12	$20	Bowl, 7-1/2" round, plain edge	$23	$35
Bowl, 4-1/2" round lily	$15	$27	Bowl, 8-1/4" celery	$18	$35
Bowl, 5-1/2" square	$15	$24	Creamer	$18	$30
Bowl, 5-1/2" 1 handle	$15	$28	Pitcher, 5-1/4", pint jug	$85	
Bowl, 6" deep round	$16	$30	Plate, 7-3/4" square	$15	$20
Bowl, 6-1/4" round	$14	$28	Plate, 8-3/4" round	$22	$30
Bowl, 6-1/2" round	$16	$28	Stemmed jelly, 4-1/2"	$12	$25
Bowl, 6-1/2" 2-handled pickle	$17	$35	Stemmed jelly, 4-1/2", flared top	$14	$27
Bowl, 6-3/4" round, unflared	$14	$25	Sugar	$20	$35
Bowl, 7-1/4" round, flared	$14	$25	Vase, 6" bouquet	$25	$35
Bowl, 7-1/2" round, fluted edges	$22	$35			

9" dinner plate with gold trim

**Hocking Glass Company, 1929-33
Colors: green, pink, yellow, crystal,
occasional pieces in satin finish**

Most commonly found in green, it is possible to collect in both yellow and pink. There are numerous block patterns, but *Block Optic* is distinguished from other block patterns in the thickness of the glass. This particular pattern manufactured by Hocking is very thin glass.

Green is the most available color while yellow is difficult to uncover in any quantity. A small number of pieces were produced in a satin or frosty finish. The items with black stems and/or bases are very difficult to find. Other scarce pieces include candlesticks, vases, mugs, and other odd pieces. There is no round butter dish to be found in *Block Optic*. Only rectangular ones have been discovered. The dinner plate often is found with a snowflake design in the center.

While *Block Optic* was not collected avidly in the beginning of the Depression glass craze, it is extremely desirable today. It seems that almost every household has a piece or two of this pattern in its cupboards. In addition, there are a great variety of pieces possible with cups in five different styles and creamers and sugars found in four different forms. With affordable prices and its very simplistic, yet elegant patterns, this tableware is very appealing to many that seek the "Country" or "Southwest" decor for their homes.

Sherbet plate, luncheon plate w/gold trim, luncheon plate without gold trim, dinner plate, berry bowl, cup and saucer, sherbet

12 ¾" plate, goblet, candy jar w/cover, candy dish, butter dish w/cover, creamer, sugar

4 ¾" tumblers and bulbous 54 oz. pitcher

9" dinner plate in pink

Goblet, stemmed sherbet, plate, cup, and 5" flat tumbler

BLOCK OPTIC, "BLOCK"

	Green	Yellow	Pink
Bowl, 4-1/4" diam., 1-3/8" tall	$9		$11
Bowl, 4-1/2" diam., 1-1/2" tall	$28		$30
Bowl, 5-1/4" cereal	$15		$28
Bowl, 7-1/4" salad	$185		
Bowl, 8-1/2" large berry	$25		$35
Bowl, 11-3/4" rolled-edge console	$75		$90
Butter dish and cover, 3"x5"	$50		
Candlesticks, 1-3/4" pr.	$100		$75
Candy jar & cover, 2-1/4" tall	$60	$70	$60
Candy jar & cover, 6-1/4" tall	$60		$135
Comport, 4" wide mayonnaise	$35		$70
Creamer	$15	$15	$15
Cup	$7	$8	$7
Goblet, 3-1/2" short wine	$400		$400
Goblet, 4" cocktail	$40		$40
Goblet, 4-1/2" wine	$40		$40
Goblet, 5-3/4", 9 oz.	$30		$35
Goblet, 7-1/4", 9 oz. thin		$40	
Ice bucket	$42		$75
Ice tub or butter tub, open	$60		$95
Mug	$35		
Pitcher, 7-5/8", 54 oz., bulbous	$70		$125
Pitcher, 8-1/2", 54 oz.	$60		$50
Pitcher, 8", 80 oz.	$90		$90
Plate, 6" sherbet	$3	$3	$3
Plate, 8" luncheon	$5	$5	$5
Plate, 9" dinner	$28	$45	$35

	Green	Yellow	Pink
Plate, 9" grill	$30	$40	$30
Plate, 10-1/4" sandwich	$35		$35
Plate, 12-3/4"	$30	$30	
Salt and pepper, ftd.	$35	$85	$80
Salt and pepper, squat style	$100		
Sandwich server, center handle	$80		$90
Saucer, 5-3/4", with cup ring	$10		$8
Saucer, 6-1/8", with cup ring	$10		$8
Sherbet, non-stemmed (cone)	$4		
Sherbet, 3-1/4", 5-1/2 oz.	$6	$10	$8
Sherbet, 4-3/4", 6 oz.	$17	$17	$17
Sugar, 3 styles, as creamer	$13	$13	$13
Tumbler, 3 oz., 2-5/8"	$25		$30
Tumbler, 5 oz., 3-1/2", flat	$25		$30
Tumbler, 9-1/2 oz. flat, 3-13/16" flat	$15		$15
Tumbler, 10 or 11 oz. 5" flat	$22		$18
Tumbler, 12 oz., 4-7/8" flat	$25		$25
Tumbler, 15 oz., flat, 5-1/4"	$50		$40
Tumbler, 3 oz., 3-1/4", ftd.	$28		$28
Tumbler, 9 oz. ftd.	$18	$22	$15
Tumbler, 6", 10 oz. ftd.	$35		$32
Tumble-up night set	$80		
Tumbler, 3" only	$50		
Bottle only	$15		
Vase, 5-3/4" blown	$350		
Whiskey, 1-5/8", 1 oz.	$40		$45
Whiskey, 2-1/4", 2 oz.	$35		$40

Bowknot

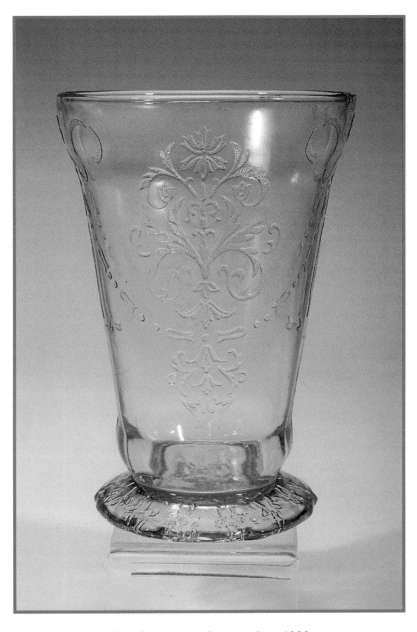

6", 10 oz. footed tumbler illustrating pattern

Manufacturer unknown, late 1920s
Colors: green, crystal

This is a difficult pattern to collect since *Bowknot* is not very abundant. To this date, there is no solid evidence available as to who manufactured this pattern. Very simple, it is a beautiful pattern, but available in only a couple of different pieces. Perhaps more will surface in years ahead.

Nonetheless, an increased interest in this pattern has driven up prices in the past few years. Even though collectors find it difficult to locate perfect pieces (inner edges often are rough), they enjoy the "lacey" pattern on this heavier, green glass.

"BOWKNOT"

	Green		Green
Bowl, 4-1/2" berry	$18	Sherbet, low ftd.	$18
Bowl, 5-1/2" cereal	$25	Tumbler, 5", 10 oz.	$24
Cup	$9	Tumbler, 5", 10 oz ftd.	$24
Plate, 7" salad	$15		

9" dinner plate

Hocking Glass Company, 1934-65
Colors: Blue, pink, crystal, red, green, white

While this pattern was started in the mid-1930s, it was manufactured well into the 1960s. Very abundant, especially in blue, this is an affordable and very beautiful pattern to collect. While the original trade name often changed as the different colors were produced over the years, most collectors refer to this pattern as *Bubble*.

Often it is also referred to as *Bullseye* and *Provincial* since this pattern was released under those names as well.

The green ("Forest Green") and crystal were issued in 1937; the Ruby Red was issued in 1963; and the pale or light blue was fist issued in 1937. Some of the more rare pieces include the creamer in blue and any flanged bowl.

Especially appealing to collectors is the ice-blue color of *Bubble*. While this pattern is available in vast quantities, prices have risen also in the past year. Most certainly, its eye-appealing sparkle has created this increased interest.

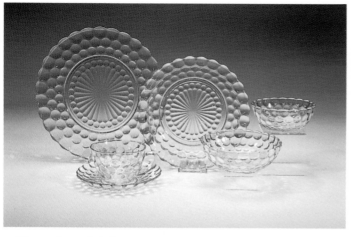

Dinner plate, salad plate, cup saucer, cereal bowl, small berry bowl

Oval platter, large round berry bowl, creamer, sugar

Green creamer and sugar, pink round berry bowl, and blue candle stick holder

"BUBBLE," "FIRE KING"

	Crystal	Blue	Red		Crystal	Blue	Red
Bowl, 4" berry	$5	$16		Plate, 9-3/8" grill		$25	
Bowl, 4-1/2" fruit	$5	$11	$8	Plate, 9-3/8" dinner	$7	$8	$15
Bowl, 5-1/4" cereal	$5	$14		Platter, 12" oval	$10	$18	
Bowl, 7-3/4" flat soup	$7	$15		Saucer	$1	$2	$8
Bowl, 8-3/8" large berry	$7	$18		Sugar	$6	$22	
Creamer	$7	$38		Tumbler, 6 oz. juice			$10
Cup	$4	$5	$9	Tumbler, 9 oz. water			$12
Pitcher, 64 oz., ice lip (red)			$60	Tumbler, 12 oz. iced tea			$15
Plate, 6-3/4", bread & butter	$2	$3		Tumbler, 16 oz. lemonade			$20

Cameo

9 ½" dinner plate

Hocking Glass Company, 1930-34
Colors: green, topaz, pink, crystal

"Ballerina" is another name often associated with this pattern since the focal point of each piece is a little dancing girl in a *Cameo*. This pattern was modeled after a Monongah Glass Company design, "Springtime." Whereas the original was plate-etched, this pattern is mold-etched.

The style might seem quite familiar to *Block Optic* collectors since many of the same blanks were used just previous to the introduction of this new pattern. Collectors will quickly see the similarities between the champagnes, wine glasses, candy jar, and glasses as well.

Cameo was one of the largest sets on the market over the years it was manufactured. Either due to its abundance or pattern-appeal, *Cameo* continues to be one of the top Depression glass patterns collected. Its affordability (with exception of very rare pieces) no doubt also contributes to its appeal. One of the most difficult pieces to locate is the center handle sandwich server. The center-ringed or cup-ringed saucers are equally difficult to locate.

Reproduction Note: Salt and peppers in pink, but with a very light to faint pattern on the shakers. Miniature children's dishes are also being created in this pattern.

Square luncheon plate, ftd. tumbler, goblet, footed sherbet, salad plate, cup, saucer, 5" tumbler, 4" tumbler, juice tumbler

Candlesticks, 12 " plate with closed handles, oval platter, oval vegetable dish, mayonnaise comport

Cake plate, divided relish dish, creamer

4", 9oz. water tumblers with 8 ½" water pitcher

5", 11 oz. flat tumblers with 8 ½" water pitcher with rope trim

Center: Cream soup bowl

Bottom right: Jam jar with cover

Bottom left: 4" low candy dish w/ cover

8" vase

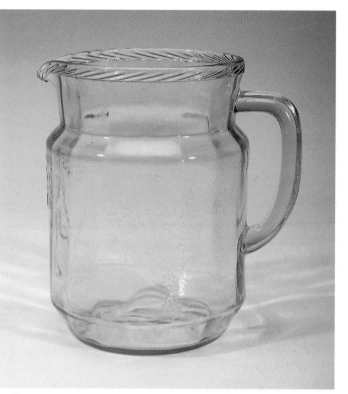

6", 36 oz. juice pitcher

Yellow grill
plate, creamer,
sugar

CAMEO, "BALLERINA," or "DANCING GIRL"

	Green	Yellow	Pink	Crystal, Plat
Bowl, 4-1/4" sauce				$8
Bowl, 4-3/4" cream soup	$140			
Bowl, 5-1/2" cereal	$35	$35	$160	$7
Bowl, 7-1/4" salad	$65			
Bowl, 8-1/4" large berry	$58		$175	
Bowl, 9" rimmed soup	$75		$135	
Bowl, 10" oval vegetable	$35	$45		
Bowl, 11", 3-legged console	$75	$95	$55	
Butter dish and cover	$240	$1600		
Cake plate, 10", 3 legs	$30			
Cake plate, 10-1/2" flat	$100		$175	
Candlesticks, 4" pr.	$110			
Candy jar, 4" low and cover	$95	$100	$500	
Candy jar, 6-1/2" tall and cover	$185			
Cocktail shaker (metal lid)				$800
Comport, 5" wide mayonnaise	$30		$200	
Cookie jar and cover	$75			
Creamer, 3-1/4"	$25	$25		
Creamer, 4-1/4"	$30		$125	
Cup, 2 styles	$14	$8	$85	$5
Decanter, 10" with stopper	$195			$250
Domino tray, 7"	$150			
Domino tray, 7" with no indentation			$240	$130
Goblet, 3-1/2" wine	$850		$900	
Goblet, 4" wine	$85		$225	
Goblet, 6" water	$65		$175	
Ice bowl or open butter, 3" tall x 5-1/2" wide	$185		$800	$265
Jam jar, 2" and cover	$195			$160
Pitcher, 5-3/4", 20 oz.	$225	$2100		
Pitcher, 6", 36 oz. juice	$70			
Pitcher, 8-1/2", 56 oz. water	$70		$1600	$550
Plate, 6" sherbet	$5	$3	$90	$2
Plate, 7" salad				$4
Plate, 8" luncheon	$10	$11	$33	$4
Plate, 8-1/2" square	$45	$250		
Plate, 9-1/2" dinner	$22	$9	$85	
Plate, 10" sandwich	$15		$42	
Plate, 10-1/2" grill	$10	$7	$50	
Plate, 10-1/2" grill with closed handles	$70	$6		
Plate, 10-1/2" with closed handles	$15	$12		
Platter, 12", closed handles	$20	$40		
Relish, 7-1/2" ftd., 3 part	$35			$160
Salt and pepper, ftd.pr.	$80		$850	
Saucer with cup ring	$195			
Saucer, 6" (sherbet plate)	$5	$3	$90	
Sherbet, 3-1/8" molded	$15	$40	$75	
Sherbet, 3-1/8" blown	$17		$75	
Sherbet, 4-7/8"	$40	$45	$100	
Sugar, 3-1/4"	$23	$18		
Sugar, 4-1/4"	$30		$125	
Tumbler, 3-3/4", 5 oz. juice	$30		$90	
Tumbler, 4", 9 oz.water	$30		$80	$9
Tumbler, 4-3/4", 10 oz. flat	$35		$95	
Tumbler, 5", 11 oz. flat	$35	$60	$95	
Tumbler, 5-1/4", 15 oz.	$75		$135	
Tumbler, 3 oz. ftd. juice	$65		$135	
Tumbler, 5", 9 oz. ftd.	$28	$16	$115	
Tumbler, 5-3/4", 11 oz. ftd.	$65		$135	
Vase, 5-3/4"	$250			
Vase, 8"	$55			

Cherry Blossom

9" dinner plate

Jeannette Glass Company, 1930-38
Colors: pink, green, delphite blue, jadite green, crystal

Cherry Blossom was one of the first mold-etched lines of glassware introduced by the Jeannette Glass Company. Quite possibly this design was inspired by the thousands of cherry trees in Washington, D.C. since many of the first advertisements for this pattern showed cherry trees blossoming by the Washington Monument.

The thick etched molding of this pattern was very popular in pink and green. The delphite blue never was as popular since the pattern did not show through quite as well as it did with the pink and green.

There is quite a bit of variations due to design changes made over the years. In the first years of production, all footed pieces had round bases. Later, they were given scalloped bases but not exclusively. The earlier pitchers were cone-shaped while the later ones were more rounded. Delphite did not appear until 1936. All the salt and pepper shakers are extremely difficult to locate. Shakers appear in pink and green only. The pink is extremely rare; so rare, that collectors have found less than six sets. Thus collectors need to realize that these shakers would be an unbelievable find.

Reproduction Note: A.A. Importing Co., Inc. has reproduced this pattern in pink, red, and green. Those pieces reissued include butter dish, tumblers, plates, cups, and saucers. Pitchers and tumblers have been made in red only. The overall pattern quality is much lower in this new reissue.

8" salad plate, divided grill plate, berry bowl, covered butter dish

6" bread and butter plate, 9" dinner plate, butter bottom

Creamer, sugar w/cover, oval vegetable bowl, 8 ½" round berry

6 ¾" pitcher with three 4 ½" tumblers

9" dinner plate in green

10 ¼" cake plate

4 ¾" berry bowl, sherbet, salad plate, dinner plate, 5 ¾" cereal bowl, cup, saucer

Oval vegetable bowl, covered butter dish, creamer, sugar bowl w/cover

8", 42 oz. flat pitcher, 4 ½" tumbler, 3 ¾" flat tumbler

CHERRY BLOSSOM

	Pink	Green	Delphite		Pink	Green	Delphite
Bowl, 4-3/4" berry	$25	$20	$20	Plate, 9" dinner	$24	$25	$20
Bowl, 5-3/4" cereal	$60	$58		Plate, 9" grill	$35	$35	
Bowl, 7-3/4" flat soup	$95	$85		Plate, 10" grill		$95	
Bowl, 8-1/2" round berry	$50	$50	$50	Platter, 11" oval	$40	$45	$45
Bowl, 9" oval vegetable	$45	$45	$50	Platter, 13" and 13" divided	$80	$80	
Bowl, 9" 2-handled	$65	$65	$25	Salt and pepper (scalloped bottom)	$1300	$1050	
Bowl, 10-1/2", 3 leg fruit	$95	$90		Saucer	$10	$10	$10
Butter dish and cover	$100	$110		Sherbet	$20	$20	$16
Cake plate (3 legs) 10-1/4"	$40	$35		Sugar	$15	$18	$18
Coaster	$15	$14		Sugar cover	$20	$20	
Creamer	$20	$20	$20	Tray, 10-1/2" sandwich	$30	$30	$22
Cup	$20	$21	$18	Tumbler, 3-3/4", 4 oz. footed AOP	$20	$22	$22
Mug, 7 oz.	$265	$195		Tumbler, 4-1/2", 9 oz. round foot AOP	$40	$40	$22
Pitcher, 6-3/4" AOP, 36 oz.	$95	$70	$85	Tumbler, 4-1/2", 8 oz. scalloped foot AOP	$35	$35	$22
Pitcher, 8" PAT, 42 oz. flat	$90	$90		Tumbler, 3-1/2", 4 oz. flat PAT	$20	$30	
Pitcher, 8" PAT, 36 oz. ftd	$70	$70		Tumbler, 4-1/4", 9 oz. flat PAT	$25	$25	
Plate, 6" sherbet	$10	$10	$12	Tumbler, 5", 12 oz.flat PAT	$65	$80	
Plate, 7" salad	$35	$30					

Cloverleaf

8" luncheon plate

**Hazel Atlas Glass Company, 1931-1935
Colors: green, pink, yellow, black, crystal**

A very simple pattern, *Cloverleaf* is more popular today than it was when it was originally manufactured, especially in black. Black glass appeals to many who are intrigued by Art Deco and its fascinating shapes. While the shapes are traditional, the color fits the Art Deco movement. Halloween collectors often use the black for accent pieces while decorating for this holiday. Black *Cloverleaf* blends extremely well with vintage German orange, yellow, and black decorations. Green *Cloverleaf* most certainly could be used for St. Patrick's Day as decorative pieces as well. While very beautiful, pink and yellow are difficult to find.

It was a very small line with only nineteen different pieces offered, based on what has been discovered by collectors thus far. Only ten have been found in black. The pattern can be found etched on both the outside as well as the inside of the piece.

Amber footed candy dish w/cover, salt and pepper shakers, luncheon plate, green sherbet, pink sherbet

8" black luncheon plate

CLOVERLEAF

	Pink	Green	Yellow	Black
Ash tray, 4", match holder in center				$70
Ash tray, 5-3/4", match holder in center				$85
Bowl, 4" dessert	$15	$22	$30	
Bowl, 5" cereal		$30	$40	
Bowl, 7" deep salad		$45	$60	
Bowl, 8"		$70		
Candy dish and cover		$65	$120	
Creamer, 3-5/8" ftd.		$10	$18	$20
Cup	$8	$9	$11	$20
Plate, 6" sherbet		$5	$8	$40
Plate, 8" luncheon	$8	$9	$15	$20
Plate, 10-1/4" grill		$22	$25	
Salt and pepper, pr.		$40	$130	$110
Saucer	$3	$3	$4	$6
Sherbet, 3" ftd.	$8	$7	$15	$25
Sugar, 3-5/8" ftd.		$10	$18	$20
Tumbler, 4", 9 oz. flat		$65		
Tumbler, 3-3/4", 10 oz. flat flared	$24	$40		
Tumbler, 5-3/4", 10 oz. ftd.		$25	$35	

Creamer, sugar, luncheon plate, cup saucer in black

Colonial Block

Sugar bowl w/cover, creamer

Hazel Atlas Glass Company, early 1930s
Colors: green, pink, crystal, black

Often confused with other block patterns, this pattern is similar to block patterns produced by U.S. Glass Company. By looking carefully at this pattern, one can see the even "squares" along with a very heavy glass. In fact, the heavy molded green and pink glass is characteristic of this pattern. The goblets and pitcher are often substituted to go with other Block patterns simply due to the durability of this glass. Actually, block patterns are quite easily interchanged in a collection and most certainly "look-alike" pieces add some contrast to a table setting.

Candy jar w/cover, sherbet

Water pitcher w/three stemmed water goblets

COLONIAL BLOCK

	Pink, Green	White
Bowl, 4"	$7	
Bowl, 7"	$20	
Butter dish	$60	
Butter tub	$50	
Candy jar w/cover	$45	
Creamer	$15	$7
Goblet	$14	
Pitcher	$50	
Powder jar with lid	$20	
Sherbet	$10	
Sugar	$10	$6
Sugar lid	$12	$5
Tumbler, 5-1/4", 5 oz., ftd.	$28	

8 ½" luncheon plate

Hocking Glass Company, 1934-38
Colors: green, pink, crystal

Some collectors refer to this pattern as "Knife and Fork," but Hocking did label this pattern as *Colonial* when originally released in 1934. A very heavy glass with larger-than-usual pieces characterizes this pattern. Its weight and size are reminiscent of early American glass used in colonial days.

It is relatively difficult to collect as there are not too many pieces available today. The "spooner" is an unusual piece in this pattern, especially considering the Depression glass era. There seem to be quite a few tumbler sizes from which to choose. Mugs are quite rare in any of the colors, but a green mug would be a prize indeed.

Green luncheon plate, pink 3 3/8" sherbet

COLONIAL, "KNIFE AND FORK"

	Pink	Green	Crystal		Pink	Green	Crystal
Bowl, 3-3/4" berry	$55			Saucer/sherbet plate	$6	$8	$4
Bowl, 4-1/2" berry	$18	$29	$12	Sherbet, 3"	$25		
Bowl, 5-1/2" cereal	$65	$95	$33	Sherbet, 3-3/8"	$12	$15	$7
Bowl, 4-1/2" cream soup	$70	$70	$65	Spoon holder or celery, 5-1/2"	$130	$125	$75
Bowl, 7" low soup	$65	$65	$28	Stem, 3-3/4", 1 oz. cordial		$30	$20
Bowl, 9" large berry	$28	$33	$25	Stem, 4", 3 oz. cocktail		$30	$20
Bowl, 10" oval vegetable	$35	$38	$22	Stem, 4-1/2", 2-1/2 oz. wine		$35	$20
Butter dish and cover	$650	$55	$40	Stem, 5-1/4", 4 oz. claret		$30	$20
Cheese dish		$225		Stem, 5-3/4", 8-1/2 oz. water		$35	$25
Cream/milk pitcher, 5", 16 oz.	$60	$25	$20	Sugar, 4-1/2"	$25	$15	$10
Cup (white $7)	$15	$15	$10	Sugar cover	$70	$25	$15
Mug, 4-1/2", 12 oz.	$550	$850		Tumbler, 3", 5 oz. juice	$20	$25	$15
Pitcher, 7", 54 oz.	$50	$55	$30	Tumbler, 4", 9 oz. water	$20	$20	$15
Pitcher, 7-3/4", 68 oz.	$65	$75	$35	Tumbler, 5-1/8" high, 11 oz.	$35	$42	$22
Plate, 6", sherbet	$6	$8	$4	Tumbler, 12 oz. iced tea	$50	$50	$24
Plate, 8-1/2" luncheon	$9	$9	$5	Tumbler, 15 oz. lemonade	$65	$75	$45
Plate, 10" dinner	$55	$65	$30	Tumbler, 3-3/4", 3 oz. ftd.	$20	$25	$13
Plate, 10" grill	$25	$25	$15	Tumbler, 4", 5 oz. ftd.	$35	$40	$22
Platter, 12" oval	$32	$22	$15	Tumbler, 5-1/4", 10 oz. ftd.	$50	$50	$27
Salt and pepper, pr.	$140	$150	$60	Whiskey, 2-1/2", 1-1/2 oz.	$15	$20	$11

Columbia

11" chop plate

Federal Glass Company, 1938-40
Colors: crystal, pink

While this pattern was first produced in pink, it quickly turned to crystal since the popularity of colored tableware was quickly fading at this time. "Hail 'Columbia'" was used in the first advertisement of this Federal pattern.

Some pieces are found with gold rims and various other color decorations, especially on butter dish covers. Federal Glass Company often sold *Columbia* in "Snack Sets." Lots of butter dishes are being found as a result of them being used by the dairy industry to promote the sale of butter. Tumblers are found in abundance as well; countless numbers were sold with cottage cheese in them. The clear color and simple pattern appealed to promoters of such dairy products.

COLUMBIA

	Crystal	Pink
Bowl, 5" cereal	$20	
Bowl, 8" low soup	$25	
Bowl, 8-1/2" salad	$25	
Bowl, 10-1/2" ruffled edge	$25	
Butter dish and cover	$20	
Cup	$9	$25
Plate, 6" bread & butter	$4	$15
Plate, 9-1/2" luncheon	$10	$35
Plate, 11" chop	$12	
Saucer	$4	$10
Snack plate	$35	
Tumbler, 2-7/8", 4 oz., juice	$35	
Tumbler, 9 oz., water	$35	

Chop plate, 10 ½" ruffled bowl

Coronation

6" sherbet plate

Hocking Glass Company, 1936
Colors: pink, crystal, ruby red

Actually a very elegant, simple pattern, the most readily found pieces are the master berry bowl and its accompanying berry dishes. This berry set was part of a promotional sales campaign, thus its availability today.

Collectors are advised not to confuse the tumblers in this pattern with *Lace Edge* pattern tumblers. This confusion often arises between dealer and buyer alike. The ray designs in the *Coronation* tumblers ascend much farther up the side than do those on the *Lace Edge* tumblers. However, *Lace Edge* collectors often will purchase *Coronation* tumblers since they are much more affordable and their "look-alike" quality blends them well with this pattern.

Ruby red is a popular color for many, especially for those who like to decorate for St. Valentine's Day and Christmas. These occasional pieces in ruby are extremely attractive when filled with candy, ornaments, or Christmas greens. The handles on the ruby red bowls are mostly open.

6" sherbet plate, cup, sherbet, 6 ½" handled nappy, 8" large handled berry bowl

CORONATION, "BANDED RIB," "SAXON"

	Pink	Royal Ruby	Green
Bowl, 4-1/4" berry, handled	$6	$8	
Bowl, 4-1/4", no handles	$75		$50
Bowl, 6-1/2" nappy, handled	$8	$15	
Bowl, 8" large berry, handled	$10	$20	
Bowl, 8", no handles	$150		$190
Cup	$6	$7	
Pitcher, 7-3/4", 68 oz.	$575		
Plate, 6", sherbet	$4		
Plate, 8-1/2" luncheon	$5	$10	$50
Saucer (same as 6" plate)	$2		
Sherbet	$5		$85
Tumbler, 5", 10 oz. ftd.	$30		$185

8" luncheon plate

Jeannette Glass Company, 1929-33
Colors: pink, green, crystal

Cubist is actually quite an important pattern, not due to its popularity with collectors today, but its distinction as one of the first of the Depression glass patterns to be manufactured by the Jeannette Glass Company. Green was quite quickly discontinued, making pink the most often found color. The candy and sugar lids are the same and are interchangeable.

This pattern is finding popularity among younger collectors who enjoy the deep cubist pattern molding. These collectors find this tableware to be a more "modern" style compatible with today's styles.

Fostoria produced a pattern similar to *Cubist* called *American,* but Fostoria's pattern was primarily produced in crystal, is made from a much higher quality glass, and is much heavier in weight.

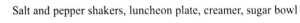

Salt and pepper shakers, luncheon plate, creamer, sugar bowl

Green 6 ½" salad bowl

CUBE, "CUBIST"

	Pink	Green		Pink	Green
Bowl, 4-1/2" dessert	$7	$8	Plate, 6" sherbet	$4	$4
Bowl, 4-1/2" deep	$9		Plate, 8" luncheon	$10	$10
Bowl, 6-1/2" salad	$10	$15	Powder jar and cover, 3 legs	$30	$28
Butter dish and cover	$70	$70	Salt and pepper, pr.	$40	$40
Candy jar and cover, 6-1/2"	$35	$40	Saucer	$3	$3
Coaster, 3-1/4"	$7	$8	Sherbet, ftd.	$7	$8
Creamer, 2-5/8"	$2		Sugar, 2-3/8	$2	
Creamer, 3-9/16"	$10	$15	Sugar, 3"	$10	$8
Cup	$9	$10	Sugar/candy cover	$15	$15
Pitcher, 8-3/4", 45 oz.	$240	$250	Tumbler, 4", 9 oz.	$70	$75

Daisy

Cup and saucer in amber

Indiana Glass Company, 1930s into the 1970s
Colors: amber, crystal, light green

Called "No. 620" in Indiana Glass Company lists, *Daisy* is the name coined by collectors. Green and milkglass are from the 1960s and 1970s; therefore not really Depression era glass. Amber was produced during the 1940s. Crystal is the most common color of this particular pattern and accurately the only Depression glass pattern since the other colors were manufactured much later.

"DAISY," NUMBER 620

	Crystal	Amber		Crystal	Amber
Bowl, 4-1/2" berry	$5	$9	Plate, 9-3/8" dinner	$6	$10
Bowl, 4-1/2" cream soup	$5	$12	Plate, 10-3/8" grill	$6	$10
Bowl, 6" cereal	$10	$35	Plate, 11-1/2", cake or sandwich	$7	$14
Bowl, 7-3/8" berry	$8	$15	Platter, 10-3/4"	$8	$18
Bowl, 9-3/8" deep berry	$13	$30	Relish dish, 3-part, 8-3/8"	$12	$35
Bowl, 10" oval vegetable	$10	$16	Saucer	$2	$3
Creamer, footed	$6	$10	Sherbet, ftd.	$5	$9
Cup	$4	$6	Sugar, ftd.	$7	$8
Plate, 6" sherbet	$2	$3	Tumbler, 9 oz. ftd.	$10	$18
Plate, 7-3/8" salad	$4	$8	Tumbler, 12 oz. ftd.	$25	$45
Plate, 8-3/8" luncheon	$5	$7			

9 ½" dinner plate

Federal Glass Company, 1937-40
Colors: pink, amber, crystal

This pattern originates much earlier than the Depression, according to company records since it carries a much earlier pattern number. However, its current familiarity as *Diana* is due to the fact that when it was reissued in 1937, a Federal employee named this pattern after his daughter, Diana. Look for the two different styles of cups: regular and demitasse.

Sometimes this pattern is confused with other swirl patterns, but a careful look at the center reveals the swirl pattern, which corresponds to the outside swirls contained on the lips of plates, cups, saucers, and bowls.

Few odd pieces were made other than the coaster, ash tray, and small demitasse set. Some frosted pieces have been discovered in recent years.

Reproduction Note: The 11-inch console bowl has been reproduced.

6 ½" bread and butter plate, cereal bowl, coaster, dinner plate, cup and saucer, water tumbler

11" console bowl, 9" salad plate, round candy jar w/cover

DIANA

	Crystal	Pink	Amber		Crystal	Pink	Amber
Ash tray, 3-1/2"	$3	$4		Plate, 6" bread & butter	$2	$4	$2
Bowl, 5" cereal	$6	$12	$15	Plate, 9-1/2"	$5	$20	$9
Bowl, 5-1/2" cream soup	$9	$25	$18	Plate, 11-3/4" sandwich	$8	$25	$10
Bowl, 9" salad	$11	$20	$25	Platter, 12" oval	$9	$30	$13
Bowl, 11" console fruit	$14	$50	$25	Salt and pepper, pr.	$45	$80	$125
Bowl, 12" scalloped edge	$14	$35	$25	Saucer	$2	$5	$2
Candy jar and cover, round	$20	$50	$45	Sherbet	$3	$12	$10
Coaster, 3-1/2"	$3	$7	$10	Sugar, open oval	$5	$15	$8
Creamer, oval	$5	$12	$9	Tumbler, 4-1/8", 9 oz.	$30	$50	$30
Cup	$3	$18	$7				
Cup, 2 oz. demitasse and 4-1/2" saucer set	$13	$45					

Dogwood

8" luncheon plate

Macbeth-Evans Company, 1928-32
Colors: pink, green, crystal

Dogwood was the first mold-etched pattern for the Macbeth Evans Company. Originally catalogued as a "B Pattern," employees recall this pattern as being referred to as only as *Dogwood*. Sometimes this pattern is referred to as *Apple Blossom* or *Wild Rose*. A characteristic of this tableware is its very thin glass. Since it was so thin, the pitcher and creamer spouts were applied by hand. A few of the pieces were quite fragile in that the glass was a bit too thin. After its quick rise in popularity, Macbeth-Evans redesigned the molds to increase the thickness of the glass in order to achieve complete machine manufacturing and make it stronger.

This pattern is especially appealing to many collectors due to the intricate, almost Japanese-style etching of the dogwood blossoms.

Some of the sectioned grill plates have been discovered with the center design absent. The large twelve-inch oval platter is at the top of the rarity chart in this pattern.

Cup and saucer, 10 ¼" fruit bowl, low footed sherbet, 5 ½" cereal bowl

DOGWOOD, "APPLE BLOSSOM," "WILD ROSE"

	Pink	Green	Monax Cremax
Bowl, 5-1/2" cereal	$35	$40	$5
Bowl, 8-1/2" berry	$75	$120	$40
Bowl, 10-1/4" fruit	$550	$250	$120
Cake plate, 13" heavy solid foot	$135	$115	$195
Coaster, 3-1/4"	$600		
Creamer, 2-1/2" thin, flat	$20	$50	
Creamer, 3-1/4" thick, footed	$22		
Cup, thick	$20		$40
Cup, thin	$18	$40	
Pitcher, 8", 80 oz. decorated	$250	$500	
Pitcher, 8", 80 oz. (American Sweetheart Style)	$650		
Plate, 6" bread and butter	$8	$9	$22
Plate, 8" luncheon	$7	$8	
Plate, 9-1/4" dinner	$40		
Plate, 10-1/2" grill	$25	$25	
Plate, 12" salver	$30		$15
Platter, 12" oval (rare)	$675		
Saucer	$6	$7	$20
Sherbet, low footed	$40	$120	
Sugar, 2-1/2" thin, flat	$18	$45	
Sugar, 3-1/4" thick, footed	$18		
Tumbler, 3-1/2", 5 oz. decorated	$300		
Tumbler, 4", 10 oz. decorated	$50	$100	
Tumbler, 4-3/4", 11 oz. decorated	$50	$110	
Tumbler, 5", 12 oz. decorated	$70	$120	
Tumbler, moulded band	$25		

Doric

Jeannette Glass Company, 1935-38
Colors: pink, green, crystal, topaz, delphite, yellow, opaque blue

Characterized by a wagon spoke design radiating from a center snowflake design, Jeannette Glass Company produced this pattern primarily in pink and green. Made of a heavier glass, Jeannette last advertised *Doric* for sale in 1938.

Pink, green, and delphite are the three colors most often found. Iridescent pieces are of recent vintage. Some very interesting pieces exist in this pattern. An eight-inch square tray which holds two four-inch and one four by eight-inch relish compartments is but one of the unique pieces.

9" dinner plate

6" bread and butter plate, 4 ½" berry bowl, creamer

Square compartment for relish tray, 5 ½" berry bowl, 5 ½" pitcher

8" luncheon plate, cup and saucer

9" dinner plate

4 ½" berry bowl, 5 ½" cereal bowl, 4", 10oz. tumblers

8 ¼" large berry bowl, 9" oval vegetable bowl

10" handled plate, 4" by 4" relish insert, creamer, sugar bowl

DORIC

	Pink	Green		Pink	Green
Bowl, 4-1/2" berry	$10	$10	Plate, 9" dinner	$18	$20
Bowl, 5-1/2" cereal	$70	$80	Plate, 9" grill	$20	$25
Bowl, 8-1/4" large berry	$30	$32	Platter, 12" oval	$25	$30
Bowl, 9" 2-handled	$30	$20	Relish tray, 4"x4"	$10	$10
Bowl, 9" oval vegetable	$35	$40	Relish tray, 4"x8"	$15	$18
Butter dish and cover	$75	$90	Salt and pepper, pr.	$45	$50
Cake plate, 10", 3 legs	$30	$30	Saucer	$4	$5
Candy dish and cover, 8"	$50	$50	Sherbet, footed	$15	$16
Candy dish, 3-part	$10	$10	Sugar	$15	$15
Coaster, 3"	$18	$18	Sugar cover	$15	$25
Creamer, 4"	$15	$16	Tray, 10" handled	$15	$18
Cup	$9	$10	Tray, 8"x8" serving	$25	$30
Pitcher, 5-1/2", 32 oz. flat	$40	$45	Tumbler, 4-1/2", 9 oz.	$85	$115
Pitcher, 7-1/2", 48 oz. footed	$700	$1105	Tumbler, 4", 10 oz. footed	$85	$105
Plate, 6" sherbet	$5	$6	Tumbler, 5", 12 oz., footed	$90	$140
Plate, 7" salad	$20	$25			

Doric and Pansy

Jeannette Glass Company, 1937-38
Colors: pink, crystal, ultramarine

When first issued, "ultra-marine" was the color chosen. This pattern is just like *Doric,* but collectors will find a flower etched on every other panel flanking the "star" design of *Doric.*

Doric and Pansy is still a difficult pattern to collect since all colors are scarce with ultramarine being the most often encountered. As with the pink color that Jeannette Glass Company produces, the ultramarine color does vary quite a bit, so collectors should not be alarmed when the colors don't exactly match. A highly sought set in *Doric and Pansy* is the child's set called "Pretty Polly Party Dishes."

DORIC AND PANSY

	Green, Teal	Pink, Crystal
Bowl, 4-1/2" berry	$20	$10
Bowl, 8" large berry	$85	$30
Bowl, 9" handled	$35	$20
Butter dish and cover	$500	
Cup	$16	$10
Creamer	$120	$80
Plate, 6" sherbet	$10	$8
Plate, 7" salad	$40	
Plate, 9" dinner	$35	$12
Salt and pepper, pr.	$400	
Saucer	$6	$7
Sugar, open	$120	$80
Tray, 10" handled	$30	
Tumbler, 4-1/2", 9 oz.	$120	
Tumbler, 4-1/4", 10 oz.	$580	

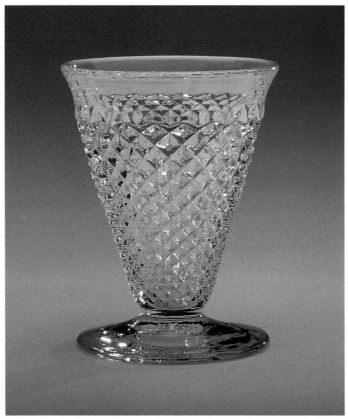

Crystal juice glass illustrating pattern

**Westmoreland Glass Company, 1925 to late 1970s
Colors: amber, pink, blue, cobalt, red, crystal, turquoise, green**

Beginning collectors often find this pattern to be the most confusing to collect, but it is also counted among the most elegant. So some simple facts can help to understand this pattern a little better.

English Hobnail was first released in 1925 in crystal and amber. In 1929-30 adding black stems to some footed pieces made a variation of crystal. Blue, green, and pink were added in 1926.

Crystal has been consistently produced from the very beginning. In the 1960s another hue of amber was added. In the 1970s even more colors were added. While the manufacturing dates do vary extensively, this pattern perhaps should be collected for its beauty rather than its age.

This pattern is similar to *Miss America*. The principal differences lie in the lengths of the rays in the center design. The rays in *Miss America* are uniform in length while those in *English Hobnail* are in varying lengths. Turquoise and cobalt usually are double in price over other pieces located.

ENGLISH HOBNAIL

	Pink or Green		Pink or Green
Ashtray, several shapes	$25	Goblet, 3 oz. cocktail	$25
Bowls, 4-1/2", 5" square & round	$15	Goblet, 6-1/4, 8 oz.	$30
Bowl, cream soup	$25	Grapefruit, 6-1/2", flange rim	$20
Bowls, 6", several styles	$18	Lamp, 6-1/4", electric	$75
Bowls, 8", several styles	$30	Lamp, 9-1/4"	$130
Bowls, 8", footed & two-handled	$85	Marmalade & cover	$40
Bowls, 11" & 12" nappies	$50	Pitcher, 23 oz.	$180
Bowls, relish, oval, 8" & 9"	$30	Pitcher, 39 oz.	$250
Bowl, relish, oval, 12"	$30	Pitcher, 60 oz.	$310
Candlesticks, 3-1/2", pr.	$40	Pitcher, 1/2 gal., straight sides	$315
Candlesticks, 8-1/2", pr.	$70	Plate, 5-1/2" & 6-1/2", sherbet	$8
Candy dish, 1/2 lb., cone shaped	$55	Plate, 7-1/4", pie	$9
Candy dish & cover, three feet	$70	Plate, 8", round or square	$12
Celery dish, 9"	$32	Plate, 10" dinner	$35
Celery dish, 12"	$35	Salt & pepper, pr., round or sq. base	$80
Cigarette box	$30	Salt dip, 2" footed w/place card holder	$25
Cologne bottle	$32	Saucer	$5
Creamer, footed or flat	$35	Sherbet	$15
Cup	$20	Sugar, footed or flat	$25
Decanter, 20 oz. w/stopper	$150	Tumbler, 3-3/4", 5 oz. or 8 oz.	$20
Demitasse cup & saucer	$70	Tumbler, 4", 10 oz. ice tea	$25
Egg cup	$40	Tumbler, 5", 12 oz. ice tea	$35
Goblet, 2 oz. wine	$30		

8 ½" dinner plate

Jeannette Glass Company, 1950
Colors: iridescent, crystal, blue, pink

Floragold is still another pattern which does not strictly fall into the Depression era of glass manufacturing. However, its machine-manufactured mold-etch process is so similar to this era that it is avidly collected by many. It blends very well with other iridescent patterns. Most difficult to locate is the vase, which looks like a large footed tumbler with a scalloped or ruffled upper edge.

15 oz. footed tumbler, 64 oz. pitcher, cup, salad plate, cereal bowl, 6 ½" ruffled plate

Candy dish, deep salad bowl, 12" large ruffled fruit bowl, creamer, sugar

FLORAGOLD, "LOUISA"

	Iridescent		Iridescent
Bowl, 4-1/2", square	$7	Pitcher, 64 oz.	$45
Bowl, 5-1/2", cereal, round	$40	Plate, 5-3/4", sherbet	$15
Bowl, 5-1/2", ruffled fruit	$9	Plate, 8-1/2", dinner	$40
Bowl, 8-1/2", square	$15	Plate or try, 13-1/2"	$20
Bowl, 9-1/2", salad, deep	$45	Indent on 13-1/2" plate	$60
Bowl, 9-1/2", ruffled	$9	Platter, 11-1/4"	$25
Bowl, 12", ruffled, large fruit	$8	Salt and pepper, plastic tops	$50
Butter dish and cover, 1/4 lb., oblong	$30	Saucer (same as sherbet plate)	$12
Butter dish and cover, round	$45	Sherbet, low footed	$15
Candlesticks, double branch, pr.	$50	Sugar	$9
Candy or cheese dish and cover, 6-3/4"	$60	Sugar lid	$12
Candy, 5-1/4", long, 4 feet	$8	Tumbler, 10 oz., footed	$25
Coaster/ashtray, 4"	$6	Tumbler, 11 oz., footed	$25
Creamer	$10	Tumbler, 15 oz., footed	$120
Cup	$7	Vase or celery	$425

9" dinner plate

Jeannette Glass Company, 1931-36
Colors: pink, green, opaque green

Actually a "passion flower" in design, this pattern was identified as *Floral,* one of Jeannette's first patterns of glassware sold. Sometimes this pattern is also referred to as *Poinsettia.* A full table service is possible including a lovely covered vegetable dish, family-sized salt and peppers, and very beautiful candlesticks. Candy lids and sugar lids are identical.

The cone-shaped pitcher and glasses are a popular style of the Jeannette Glass Company. Some of the last pieces produced in *Floral* were in Jadite.

Reproduction Note: salt and pepper shakers in all three colors

Footed sherbet, 4" berry bowl, dinner plate, cup and saucer

8" footed pitcher, creamer, sugar bowl w/ cover, 2-part oval relish dish, 8" covered vegetable bowl

Oval platter, sherbet plate, 5 oz. footed juice glass

10 ¼" lemonade pitcher, 5 ¼" footed lemonade glasses

Above: 9" dinner plate

Top right: Dinner plate, cup and saucer

Center right: 10 ¾" oval vegetable platter and 8" salad plate

Below: Sugar bowl w/cover, creamer, oval vegetable bowl, 8" covered vegetable dish

5 ½" pitcher with two 3 ½" footed juice tumblers

8" footed cone pitcher with 4 ¾" footed water tumblers

FLORAL, "POINSETTIA"

	Pink	Green	Delphite		Pink	Green	Delphite
Bowl, 4" berry (ruffled $65)	$25	$25	$50	Platter, 10-3/4" oval	$18	$20	$150
Bowl, 5-1/2" cream soup	$750	$750		Platter, 11"	$85		
Bowl, 7-1/2" salad (ruffled $150)	$25	$26	$60				
Bowl, 8" covered vegetable	$40	$50	$75	Refrigerator dish and cover,			
Bowl, 9" oval vegetable	$20	$23		5" square		$65	$65
Butter dish and cover	$120	$125		Relish dish, 2-part oval	$18	$20	$160
Candlesticks, 4" pr.	$90	$100		Salt and pepper, 4" ftd. pr.	$50	$55	
Candy jar and cover	$55	$55		Salt and pepper, 6" flat	$60		
Creamer, flat (Cremax $160)	$15	$16	$78	Saucer	$12	$14	
Coaster, 3-1/4"	$17	$12		Sherbet	$18	$20	$85
Comport, 9"	$800	$950		Sugar (Cremax $160)	$10	$12	$73
Cup	$13	$14		Sugar/candy cover	$15	$18	
Dresser set		$1350		Tray, 6" square, closed handles	$18	$20	
Ice tub, 3-1/2" high oval	$850	$895		Tray, 9-1/4" oval for dessert set		$210	
Lamp	$280	$290		Tumbler, 3-1/2", 3 oz. ftd.		$180	
Pitcher, 5-1/2", 23 or 24 oz.		$595		Tumbler, 4", 5 oz. ftd. juice	$20	$25	
Pitcher, 8", 32 oz. ftd. cone	$50	$50		Tumbler, 4-1/2", 9 oz. flat		$190	
Pitcher, 10-1/4", 48 oz. lemonade	$300	$320		Tumbler, 4-3/4", 7 oz. ftd. water	$20	$25	$195
Plate, 6" sherbet	$7	$8		Tumbler, 5-1/4", 9 oz. ftd. lemonade	$50	$55	
Plate, 8" salad	$10	$12		Vase, 3 legged rose bowl		$550	
Plate, 9" dinner	$18	$19	$150	Vase, 3 legged flared (also in crystal)		$500	
Plate, 9" grill		$250		Vase, 6-7/8" tall (8 sided)		$460	

Saucer illustrating pattern with serrated edging

Hazel Atlas Glass Company, 1932-34
Colors: green, yellow, white, crystal, dark blue

Often also referred to as *Poppy #1*, this very deeply etched design has pieces with serrated edges and bases. Many of the pieces have hexagonal shapes. Watch for those hexagon shapes which are characteristic of this particular pattern. Many of the items in the line are flanged and flat-rimmed with five distinct sides.

Creamer, cup and saucer, cream soup bowl, juice tumbler, footed sherbet

Cup and saucer, 5 ¼" iced tea glass, 4" straight tumbler

FLORENTINE NO. 1, "OLD FLORENTINE," "POPPY NO. 1"

	Crystal, Green	Yellow	Pink	Cobalt Blue
Ash tray, 5-1/2"	$25	$30	$30	
Bowl, 5" berry	$14	$15	$15	$20
Bowl, 5" cream soup or ruffled nut	$24		$20	$60
Bowl, 6" cereal	$22	$25	$25	
Bowl, 8-1/2" large berry	$30	$35	$35	
Bowl, 9-1/2" oval vegetable and cover	$55	$65	$65	
Butter dish and cover	$140	$180	$180	
Coaster/ash tray, 3-3/4"	$18	$20	$25	
Comport, 3-1/2", ruffled	$40		$15	$65
Creamer	$10	$18	$17	
Creamer, ruffled	$45		$40	$65
Cup	$10	$11	$10	$85
Pitcher, 6-1/2", 36 oz. ftd.	$50	$55	$55	$900
Pitcher, 7-1/2", 48 oz. flat, ice lip or none	$75	$200	$135	
Plate, 6" sherbet	$7	$8	$7	
Plate, 8-1/2" salad	$8	$12	$11	
Plate, 10" dinner	$16	$25	$25	
Plate, 10" grill	$14	$16	$25	
Platter, 11-1/2" oval	$20	$25	$25	
Salt and pepper, ftd.	$40	$60	$60	
Saucer	$4	$5	$5	$17
Sherbet, 3 oz. ftd.	$10	$12	$12	
Sugar	$10	$15	$15	
Sugar cover	$18	$30	$30	
Sugar, ruffled	$35		$35	$55
Tumbler, 3-1/4", 4 oz. ftd.	$20			
Tumbler, 3-3/4", 5 oz. ftd. juice	$20	$30	$40	
Tumbler, 4", 9 oz., ribbed	$20		$25	
Tumbler, 4-3/4", 10 oz. ftd. water	$25	$26	$26	
Tumbler, 5-1/4", 12 oz. ftd. iced tea	$30	$35	$35	
Tumbler, 5-1/4", 9 oz. lemonade (like Floral)			$150	

Salt and pepper shakers, gravy boat and platter, sugar bowl

4" footed tumblers with 7 ½" pitcher

Hazel Atlas Glass Company, 1934-36
Colors: pink, green, yellow, crystal, cobalt

Often referred to as *Poppy #2,* this pattern has the same etch-mold pattern as *Old Florentine,* but most pieces are round, and the edges of plates are smooth as are the bases of the footed pieces. Watch for those round shapes which are characteristic of this particular pattern. Only the pitchers in this pattern match *Florentine #1.*

The rarest color includes cobalt pieces.

Pair of candlesticks

Crystal salt and pepper,
sherbet, coffee cup

10" three part
relish dish

FLORENTINE NO. 2, "POPPY NO. 2"

	Crystal, Green	Pink	Yellow
Bowl, 4-1/2" berry	$14	$18	$22
Bowl, 4-3/4" cream soup	$14	$16	$22
Bowl, 5-1/2"	$33		$42
Bowl, 6" cereal	$30		$40
Bowl, 7-1/2" shallow			$95
Bowl, 8" large berry	$30	$35	$35
Bowl, 9" oval vegetable and cover	$60		$75
Bowl, 9" flat	$30		
Butter dish and cover	$140		$160
Candlesticks, 2-3/4" pr.	$50		$70
Candy dish and cover	$100	$135	$155
Coaster, 3-1/4"	$14	$16	$22
Coaster/ash tray, 3-3/4"	$18		$30
Coaster/ash tray, 5-1/2"	$18		$38
Comport, 3-1/2", ruffled	$40	$15	
Creamer	$8		$10
Cup (amber $50)	$8		$10
Custard cup or jello	$70		$90
Gravy boat			$60
Pitcher, 6-1/4", 24 oz. cone-ftd.			$190
Pitcher, 7-1/2", 28 oz. cone-ftd.	$32		$30
Pitcher, 7-1/2", 48 oz.	$80	$150	$200
Pitcher, 8-1/4", 76 oz.	$125	$240	$460
Plate, 6" sherbet	$5		$7
Plate, 6-1/4" with indent	$18		$30
Plate, 8-1/2" salad	$9	$9	$10
Plate, 10" dinner	$15		$15
Plate, 10-1/4" grill	$12		$14
Plate, 10-1/4" grill w/cream soup ring	$35		
Platter, 11" oval	$18	$18	$25
Platter, 11-1/2" for gravy boat			$45
Relish dish, 10", 3 part or plain	$20	$25	$30
Salt and pepper, pr.	$50		$55
Saucer (amber $15)	$4		$5
Sherbet, ftd. (amber $40)	$10		$11
Sugar	$10		$11
Sugar cover	$15		$25
Tray, rnd., condiment for shakers, crmr/sugar			$90
Tumbler, 3-3/8", 5 oz. juice	$15	$15	$25
Tumbler, 3-1/2", 6 oz. blown	$20		
Tumbler, 4", 9 oz. water	$15	$20	$25
Tumbler, 5", 12 oz. blown	$20		
Tumbler, 5", 12 oz. tea	$40		$60
Tumbler, 3-1/4", 5 oz. ftd.	$15	$20	
Tumbler, 4", 5 oz. ftd.	$18		$20
Tumbler, 4-1/2", 9 oz. ftd.	$30		$40
Vase or parfait, 6"	$35		$65

9" Square luncheon plate

Anchor-Hocking Glass Corporation, 1950-67
Colors: dark green

Obviously *Forest Green* is not technically a Depression pattern by the years noted above, but its extreme popularity among collectors dictates that it be included in this book. Very soon after Hocking Glass acquired the Anchor Cap and Closure Company, they introduced this particular pattern. Many of Hocking's molds used in the manufacture of Royal Ruby were used. Most of the pieces in both patterns are identical. Square pieces were introduced later than the round shapes. Each of the square pieces has a ribbed design in the center. The other items have little or no ornamentation. The vibrant green color is a perennial favorite of countless collectors.

FOREST GREEN

Ash tray	$5
Bowl, 4-3/4"	$5
Bowl, 6"	$10
Bowl, 7-1/4"	$10
Creamer	$5
Cup	$10
Mixing bowls, 3 piece set	$35
Mixing bowls, no lip or spout	$15
Pitcher, 22 oz.	$40
Pitcher, 3 qt.	$35
Plate, 6-1/2"	$5
Plate, 8-1/2"	$8
Plate, 10"	$25
Platter, rectangular	$35
Punch bowl with stand	$40
Punch cup	$5
Saucer	$3
Sugar	$5
Tumblers, 2 sizes	$8
Vase, ball-type	$10
Vase, 6-1/2"	$10
Vase, 9"	$15

Square platter, luncheon plate, creamer, sugar bowl, cup and saucer

7 ¾" salad bowl, illustrating pattern

Hocking Glass Company, 1936-37
Colors: pink crystal

Much of this pattern was produced as a promotional glassware for cereal companies. Thus there are not many pieces available to collectors. The eight-inch plates are the most difficult to locate.

4 ½" handled bowl, candy dish and cover

FORTUNE,

	Pink, Crystal
Bowl, 4" berry	$8
Bowl, 4-1/2" dessert	$10
Bowl, 4-1/2" handled	$10
Bowl, 5-1/4" rolled edge	$15
Bowl, 7-3/4" salad or large berry	$20
Candy dish and cover, flat	$25
Cup	$6
Plate, 6" sherbet	$4
Plate, 8" luncheon	$25
Saucer	$4
Tumbler, 3-1/2", 5 oz. juice	$10
Tumbler, 4", 9 oz. water	$15

9" salad plate

Hazel Atlas Glass Company and others, 1931-35
Colors: green, pink, crystal, iridescent

The design of this tableware consists of grapes, cherries, and pears. The cherry motif in the bottom of the pieces is the same as the bottom of the *Cherry Blossom* pattern.

Eleven different pieces are known to exist. Since several different companies produced the pattern, the fruits do vary somewhat. The most desirable tumblers are the older ones, which bear the cherry molding only. Some iridescent pieces are surfacing.

FRUITS,

	Green	Pink
Bowl, 5" berry	$33	$25
Bowl, 8" berry	$80	$45
Cup	$8	$7
Pitcher, 7" flat bottom	$90	
Plate, 8" luncheon	$8	$8
Saucer	$7	$5
Sherbet	$10	$8
Tumbler, 3-1/2" juice	$50	$40
Tumbler, 4" (1 fruit)	$20	$18
Tumbler, 4" (combination of fruits)	$30	$25
Tumbler, 5", 12 oz.	$150	$150

Salad plate and cup

9 ¼" dinner plate

Federal Glass Company, 1931-35
Colors: green, crystal, amber

Often referred to as *Love Birds* by collectors, *Georgian* was the pattern name in Federal's glass catalogs. In the 1920s there was a great interest in Orientalia; thus bird designs were quite popular. Upon close scrutiny, the little love birds are somewhat easily detected. Be sure to look for the basket part of the motif which often appears on pieces as well.

First produced in full dinner sets, it was later produced in luncheon sets only. There is much available in this pattern as it was a favorite promotional item. Dinner plates are found with the full design and also with the edge design (no center design and no love birds or baskets). The tumblers have baskets only in their design and the lids of the sugars have only the lace edge design present. The other covered pieces have complete lid designs.

One of the more unusual pieces is the wooden lazy Susan, 18 ¼-inches in diameter. It has seven sections in which the six-inch hot plate dishes are to be set.

5 ¾" cereal bowl, 4 ½" berry bowl, dinner plate, bread and butter plate, creamer, sugar bowl

Footed sherbet, dinner plate, bread and butter plate, cup and saucer

Covered sugar bowl, butter dish w/cover

GEORGIAN, "LOVEBIRDS,"

	Green		Green
Bowl, 4-1/2" berry	$10	Plate, 6" sherbet	$8
Bowl, 5-3/4" cereal	$25	Plate, 8" luncheon	$9
Bowl, 6-1/2" deep	$70	Plate, 9-1/4" dinner	$30
Bowl, 7-1/2" large berry	$65	Plate, 9-1/4" center design only	$25
Bowl, 9" oval vegetable	$65	Platter, 11-1/2" closed-handled	$70
Butter dish and cover	$85	Saucer	$4
Butter dish bottom	$45	Sherbet	$12
Butter dish top	$35	Sugar, 3", ftd.	$12
Cold cuts server, 18-1/2" wood		Sugar, 4", ftd.	$15
with seven 5" openings for 5" coasters	$850	Sugar cover for 3"	$40
Creamer, 3", ftd.	$15	Sugar cover for 4"	$180
Creamer, 4", ftd.	$20	Tumbler, 4", 9 oz. flat	$60
Cup	$12	Tumbler, 5-1/4", 12 oz. flat	$120
Hot Plate, 5" center design	$50		

5" tumblers illustrating pattern

Jeannette Glass Company, 1928-32
Colors: green, pink, ultramarine, iridescent

Honeycomb resembles many of the hexagon type patterns of other companies, but a heavier type glass characterizes this pattern with a distinct motif on the bottoms of most pieces.

Known by both *Hex Optic* and *Honeycomb*, the honeycomb design of this heavy type glassware appeals especially to those who collect kitchen style glassware for decorating homes. Especially prevalent are tumblers in the iridescent color since they were premiums for "Big Jo" flour and other commercial products in the 1950s and 1960s.

Green, pink, and ultramarine are the true depression colors with iridescent being produced much later.

HEX OPTIC, "HONEYCOMB,"

	Pink, Green		Pink, Green
Bowl, 4-1/4" ruffled berry	$6	Plate, 8" luncheon	$6
Bowl, 7-1/2" large berry	$8	Platter, 11" round	$15
Bowl, 7-1/4" mixing	$12	Refrigerator dish, 4"x4"	$10
Bowl, 8-1/4" mixing	$18	Refrigerator stack set, 4 pc.	$70
Bowl, 9" mixing	$25	Salt and pepper, pr.	$30
Bowl, 10" mixing	$25	Saucer	$3
Bucket reamer	$60	Sugar, 2 styles of handles	$6
Butter dish and cover, rectangular 1 lb.size	$90	Sugar shaker	$215
Creamer, 2 style handles	$6	Sherbet, 5 oz. ftd.	$5
Cup, 2 style handles	$5	Tumbler, 3-3/4", 9 oz.	$5
Ice bucket, metal handle	$18	Tumbler, 5", 12 oz.	$8
Pitcher, 5", 32 oz. sunflower motif in bottom	$22	Tumbler, 4-3/4", 7 oz. ftd.	$9
Pitcher, 9", 48 oz. ftd.	$45	Tumbler, 5-3/4" ftd.	$10
Pitcher, 8", 70 oz. flat	$225	Tumbler, 7" ftd.	$12
Plate, 6" sherbet	$3	Whiskey, 2", 1 oz.	$10

9" dinner plate

Jeannette Glass Company, 1947-49
Colors: pink, shell pink, opaque white

While this pattern was produced later, its color places it into the category of Depression glass. *Holiday* was fashioned from earlier *Windsor* molds. Once cleaned, this faceted pattern just sparkles like a diamond. Due to this sparkle,

Holiday appeals to many more collectors than it did a few years ago.

Pink is by far the most commonly found and collected color. Some white and iridescent pieces were produced in later years. Two different types of cups are found in this pattern.

Footed sherbet, berry bowl, dinner plate, cup and saucer, bread and butter plate, flat tumbler, 4" footed tumbler

13 ¾" chop plate, oval platter, large berry bowl

Creamer, sugar, butter dish w/cover, candlestick

HOLIDAY, "BUTTON AND BOWS,"

	Pink
Bowl, 5-1/8" berry	$14
Bowl, 7-3/4" soup	$60
Bowl, 8-1/2" large berry	$25
Bowl, 9-1/2" oval vegetable	$25
Bowl, 10-3/4" console	$120
Butter dish and cover	$45
Cake plate, 10-1/2" 3-legged	$95
Candlesticks, 3" pr.	$110
Creamer, ftd.	$8
Cup, two sizes	$8
Pitcher, 4-3/4", milk, 16 oz.	$60
Pitcher, 6-3/4", 52 oz.	$35

	Pink
Plate, 6" sherbet	$7
Plate, 9" dinner	$18
Plate, 13-3/4" chop	$100
Platter, 11-3/8" oval	$25
Sandwich tray, 10-1/2"	$20
Saucer, two style	$5
Sherbet	$6
Sugar	$15
Sugar cover	$18
Tumbler, 4", 10 oz. flat	$25
Tumbler, 4", ftd.	$45
Tumbler, 6", ftd.	$135

4" footed tumbler with sugar bowl

Jeannette Glass Company, 1938-40
Colors: pink, crystal

Also dubbed *Fine Ribbed,* this pattern is characterized by the waffle-like pattern easily distinguishable on the plate. This pattern is also very elegant once the fine ribs are carefully brushed and cleaned.

There are some rare pieces in this pattern including the large (96-ounce) pitcher. This pitcher does not have the char-acteristic waffle-like center, only the fine ribbing design. The tea set is also very desirable. The entire set of 14 items would fetch a commanding price. It is called "Homespun Tea Set" and is often referred to as a child's tea set.

HOMESPUN, "FINE RIB,"

Pink, Crystal

Bowl, 4-1/2", closed handles	$12
Bowl, 5" cereal, closed handles	$30
Bowl, 8-1/4" large berry	$25
Butter dish and cover	$60
Coaster/ash tray	$7
Creamer, ftd.	$11
Cup	$12
Plate, 6" sherbet	$8
Plate, 9-1/4" dinner	$20
Platter, 13", closed handles	$20
Saucer	$5
Sherbet, low flat	$18

Pink, Crystal

Sugar, ftd.	$10
Tumbler, 3-7/8", 7 oz. straight	$25
Tumbler, 4-1/8", 8 oz. water, flared top	$25
Tumbler, 4-1/4", 9 oz. band at top	$25
Tumbler, 4-5/16", 9 oz., no band	$30
Tumbler, 5-3/8", 12-1/2 oz. iced tea	$33
Tumbler, 5-7/8", 13-1/2 oz. iced tea, banded at top	$34
Tumbler, 4", 5 oz. ftd.	$8
Tumbler, 6-1/4", 15 oz. ftd.	$30
Tumbler, 6-3/8", 15 oz. ftd.	$30

Iris and Herringbone

9" dinner plate

Jeannette Glass Company, 1928-32, 1950-70
Colors: crystal, iridescent amber, pink, green, light blue

Characterized by a bouquet of iris blossoms and leaves, this pattern is characterized by very heavy glass. Once the glass is cleaned and carefully brushed in the herringbone weave in the background of the pattern, the glass sparkles like diamonds.

The iridescent (or Carnival-type) glass is especially appropriate for Halloween decorations. *Iris* was reissued for a short period in 1969 in crystal as well as in white. However the white candy dish has no design on the bottom as the old ones do. The 7 ½" soup in crystal is very rare as well as the coasters which command extremely high prices. Dinner plates in the 8-inch and 9-inch size are also quite difficult to locate.

9" dinner plate, cup and saucer, 4" flat tumbler, cup and saucer, 2 ½" low sherbet

11 ½" ruffled fruit bowl, 9 ½" ruffled fruit bowl, and 5" ruffled sauce bowl

Covered sugar bowl, creamer, butter dish w/ cover

11 ¾" sandwich plate, coaster, candlestick holder

5 ½", 8oz. goblet, 4" wine goblet, 5 ½" 4 oz. goblet

Footed pitcher with 6 ½" footed tumblers

Iridescent 9" ruffled bowl, sugar bowl w/cover,
creamer, 2 ½" low footed sherbet

IRIS, "IRIS AND HERRINGBONE,"

	Crystal	Iridescent		Crystal	Iridescent
Bowl, 4-1/2" berry, beaded edge	$50	$10	Goblet, 4-1/2", 4 oz. cocktail	$30	
Bowl, 5", ruffled, sauce	$10	$30	Goblet, 4-1/2", 3 oz. wine	$19	
Bowl, 5" cereal	$140		Goblet, 5-1/2", 4 oz.	$30	$200
Bowl, 7-1/2" soup	$180	$70	Goblet, 5-1/2", 8 oz.	$30	$200
Bowl, 8" berry, beaded edge	$90	$30	Pitcher, 9-1/2", ftd.	$40	$45
Bowl, 9-1/2", ruffled salad	$14	$14	Plate, 5-1/2", sherbet	$18	$15
Bowl, 11-1/2", ruffled fruit	$18	$15	Plate, 8" luncheon	$120	
Bowl, 11", fruit, straight edge	$60		Plate, 9" dinner	$60	$50
Butter dish and cover	$50	$45	Plate, 11-3/4" sandwich	$35	$35
Candlesticks, pr.	$50	$50	Saucer	$12	$11
Candy jar and cover	$160		Sherbet, 2-1/2", ftd.	$30	$20
Coaster	$125		Sherbet, 4", ftd.	$30	$200
Creamer, ftd.	$15	$15	Sugar	$15	$15
Cup	$25	$15	Sugar cover	$17	$17
Demitasse cup	$40	$160	Tumbler, 4", flat	$150	
Demitasse saucer	$150	$250	Tumbler, 6", ftd.	$20	$18
Fruit or nut set	$75		Tumbler, 6-1/2", ftd.	$40	
Goblet, 4" wine		$35	Vase, 9"	$30	$28

Batter bowl, creamer w/cover, sugar bowl

Jeannette Glass Company, 1936-38
Colors: jadite green

Jadite is a color as well as a pattern of kitchen-type glassware produced by Jeannette Glass Company. In addition to utilitarian pieces such as refrigerator dishes, mixing bowls, and measuring cups; a matching set of dinnerware was made, called *Jane-Ray*. Most all of these pieces were made in delphite as well. However, it would be wrong for collectors to label these blue dishes as Jadite.

JADITE

Ashtray, 5-3/4"	$15
Bowl, 4-3/4"	$6
Bowl, 5-7/8"	$10
Bowl, batter	$30
Bowl, leaf, handle	$10
Bowl, vegetable, 8-1/4"	$10
Butter, cover, 1/4 lb.	$50
Canister, coffee, 7-1/2"	$80
Cup after dinner	$10
Cup, coffee, 7 oz.	$5
Cup, St. Dennis	$7
Cup and saucer	$8
Egg cup	$15
Egg tray	$18

Refrigerator dish w/cover

Salad plate on right, illustrating pattern with plain jadite dinner plate on left

Jeannette Glass Company, 1945-63
Colors: jadite green

Although *Jane-Ray* is a rather plain pattern with a ribbed edge, its simple color and design appeal to quite a few collectors. Kitchenware in this same color was meant to accompany this dinnerware.

JANE-RAY

Grill plate	$10
Mixing bowl, 5"	$8
Mixing bowl, 6-1/2"	$10
Mixing bowl, 7"	$15
Mixing bowl, 9"	$15
Mixing bowl, straight sides, 9 x4"	$20
Mug, coffee, 7 oz.	$15
Pitcher, batter	$15
Pitcher, milk, 20 oz.	$20
Plate, 7"	$10
Plate, 9"	$8
Platter, oval, 9-1/2"	$8
Relish, 3 sections	$15
Salt shaker, 5"	$9
Saucer	$3
Shaving mug, 8 oz.	$25
Water dispenser, 11 x4-1/2"	$210

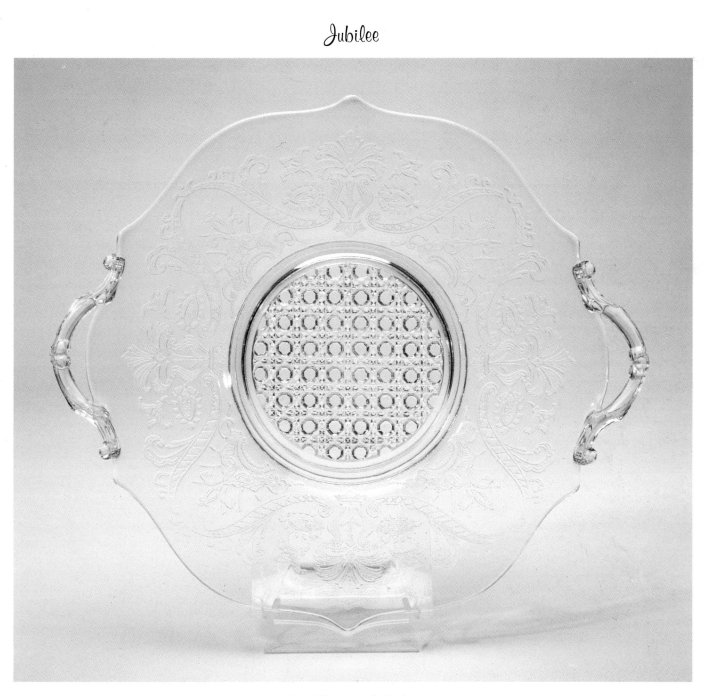

Yellow 11" two-handled cake tray

Lancaster Glass Company, 1928-34
Colors: yellow, crystal, pink

While this does appear to be a finer glass than what is commonly dubbed "Depression glass," *Jubilee* is included because when introduced it was machine-made and quite inexpensive.

A fascinating element of this glass is that the etchings vary greatly; thus many different etchings are possible to blend together. Also many pieces were produced without any ornamentation at all. This means that collectors can diversify their collection of *Jubilee* in some very interesting styles. The rarest item in this pattern is the three-piece mayonnaise set consisting of plate, bowl, and serving spoon. The spoon is almost impossible to locate.

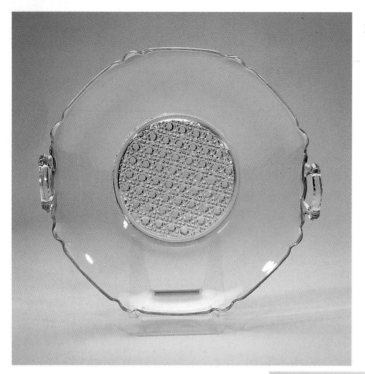

Pink 9" handled fruit bowl-top view

Pink 9" handled fruit bowl-side view

JUBILEE,

	Pink	Yellow
Bowl, 8", 3-ftd., 5-1/8" high	$250	$200
Bowl, 9" handled fruit		$125
Bowl, 11-1/2", flat fruit	$200	$170
Bowl, 11-1/2", 3-ftd.	$250	$250
Bowl, 11-1/2", 3-ftd., curved in		$225
Bowl, 13", 3-ftd.	$250	$225
Candlestick, pr.	$195	$195
Candy jar, w/lid, 3-ftd.	$325	$325
Cheese & cracker set	$255	$250
Creamer	$40	$20
Cup	$45	$15
Mayonnaise & plate	$295	$250
w/original ladle	$310	$265

	Pink	Yellow
Plate, 7" salad	$25	$15
Plate, 8-3/4" luncheon	$30	$15
Plate, 13-1/2" sandwich, handled	$85	$50
Plate, 14", 3-ftd.		$210
Saucer, two styles	$15	$5
Sherbet, 3", 8 oz.		$70
Sugar	$40	$20
Tray, 11", 2-handled cake	$65	$45
Tumbler, 5", 6 oz., ftd. juice		$100
Tumbler, 6", 10 oz., water	$85	$40
Tumbler, 6-1/8", 12-1/2 oz., iced tea		$160
Tray, 11", center-handled sandwich	$195	$200

9" mixing bowl, $25, 6" mixing bowl, $20, 4" mixing bowl, $15

Measuring pitcher, $25, two measuring cups, $35 ea., batter measuring pitcher, $40

**McKee, Hazel Atlas, Jeannette, Hocking, and others
Colors: crystal, pink, green, blue, white, jadite**

Books have been devoted to kitchenware of various types produced during the Depression years; however, that would be impossible here. Instead, here is an assortment of different items which should give collectors some general awareness of the great number of items available in this area. Many of these items were premiums as well as promotional advertising items for U.S. manufacturers attempting to boost their sales during the lean Depression years.

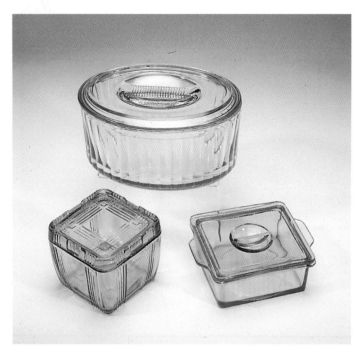

Assorted square and oval covered refrigerator dishes, $15-20 ea.

Utility pitcher, $35, 9" mixing bowl, $40, juice reamer, $50

9" mixing bowl in blue, $40, with cereal milk pitcher, $25

Large blue ribbed-water or milk
pitcher, $65

"Ships" mixing bowls made by McKee Glass Company, $25-50 ea.

Lace Edge

10 ½" dinner plate

Hocking Glass Company, 1935-38
Colors: pink, crystal,

Open Lace is another common title for this very popular pattern, first issued in 1935. *Old Colony* is the official company trade name for this pattern, but most collectors over the years have come to know this as *Lace Edge*.

This can be a confusing pattern, especially when searching for the cups, creamers, sugars, and footed tumblers. Collectors need to look for the ribbed design along with the distinctive base. The characteristic lace edge of this pattern is not incorporated into cups, creamers, sugars, or tumblers.

This is also a difficult pattern due to the easily broken edges of the open loops at the ends of bowls, plates, etc. Very few pieces were produced in crystal. Hocking also produced some pieces in a "frosted" or "satin" finish, but they generally only fetch about half of the prices listed for the pattern pieces below.

Dinner plate, salad
plate, cup and saucer

Cookie jar and cover,
9 ½" bowl, flower
bowl

Ribbed creamer and
4 ½" flat tumbler

"LACE EDGE," "OPEN LACE,"

	Pink		**Pink**
Bowl, 6-3/8" cereal	$25	Plate, 7-1/4" salad	$25
Bowl, 7-3/4" ribbed salad	$50	Plate, 8-1/4" luncheon	$25
Bowl, 8-1/4" (crystal)	$14	Plate, 10-1/2" dinner	$35
Bowl, 9-1/2", plain	$26	Plate, 10-1/2" grill	$22
Bowl, 9-1/2", ribbed	$30	Plate, 10-1/2", 3-part relish	$25
Bowl, 10-1/2", 3 legs	$260	Plate, 13", solid lace	$45
Butter dish or bon bon with cover	$70	Plate, 13", 4-part solid lace	$45
Candlesticks, pr. (frosted $85)	$270	Platter, 12-3/4"	$40
Candy jar and cover, ribbed	$50	Platter, 12-3/4", 5-part	$35
Comport, 7"	$25	Relish dish, 7-1/2", 3-part deep	$70
Comport, 7" and cover, ftd.	$50	Saucer	$12
Comport, 9"	$800	Sherbet, ftd.	$110
Cookie jar and cover (frosted $50)	$75	Sugar	$25
Creamer	$25	Tumbler, 3-1/2", 5 oz. flat	$120
Cup	$30	Tumbler, 4-1/2", 9 oz. flat	$30
Fish bowl, 1 gal. 8 oz. (crytal only)	$35	Tumbler, 5", 10-1/2 oz. ftd.	$80
Flower bowl, crystal frog	$25		

10 ¼" dinner plate

Indiana Glass Company, 1929-32
Colors: green, yellow, crystal

Collectors quickly fall in love with the basket motif of this pattern. This was Indiana Glass Company's first mold-etched pattern. Often it is confused with earlier pattern glass due to the roughness of its finish. The square plates, bowls, sugar, and creamer add to the charm of this pattern.

Yellow is the most commonly found color but still very difficult to locate if one is attempting to amass a complete set. One of the more difficult pieces to locate is the 10 ¼" dinner plate in yellow. Rarer still is the deep 8-inch bowl.

LORAIN, "BASKET," No. 615,

	Crystal, Green	Yellow		Crystal, Green	Yellow
Bowl, 6" cereal	$50	$70	Plate, 10-1/4" dinner	$50	$60
Bowl, 7-1/4" salad	$50	$70	Platter, 11-1/2"	$30	$45
Bowl, 8" deep berry	$110	$155	Relish, 8", 4-part	$18	$35
Bowl, 9-3/4" oval vegetable	$45	$55	Saucer	$5	$7
Creamer, ftd.	$18	$28	Sherbet, ftd.	$25	$35
Cup	$12	$15	Snack tray, crystal/trim	$24	
Plate, 5-1/2" sherbet	$8	$12	Sugar, ftd.	$18	$25
Plate, 7-3/4" salad	$10	$20	Tumbler, 4-3/4", 9 oz. ftd.	$25	$35
Plate, 8-3/8" luncheon	$18	$28			

Madrid

10 ½" dinner Plate

Federal Glass Company, 1932-38
Colors: amber, pink, blue, pink, crystal, green

Collectors might recognize the shapes of some of these pieces since the molds were made from *Parrot* pattern molds that did not fare too well on the market. The original line of this pattern was very large, but many new pieces were added in succeeding years. Even though the most abundantly found color is amber, "Springtime Green" was the first color produced in 1932. Due to difficulty in producing the blue color, it was soon discontinued. The last catalog illustrations of Madrid appeared in 1938.

The larger size pitchers in crystal, green, and amber are prized items, but the most difficult piece to locate is the lazy Susan in wood with the seven hot plate coasters fitted. Collectors should note that cups are found with the ribbing inside or out.

Reproduction Note: The first reproduction occurred during our Bicentennial and is easily identified by the presence of a small "76" molded onto the back of each piece. All of these were produced in amber, but a darker amber than previously produced. Fourteen pieces were manufactured as part of this Bicentennial set. In 1982, Indiana Glass Company, who purchased Federal's molds, reproduced the entire line in crystal.

Bread and butter plate, salad plate, dinner plate, cup and saucer

Creamer, sugar, butter dish w/ cover, cookie jar w/lid

Oval vegetable bowl, low console bowl, 9 ½" deep salad bowl

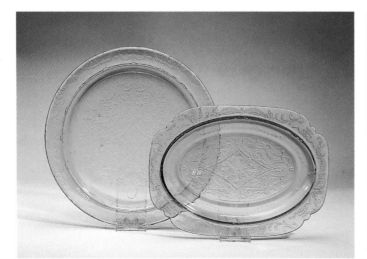

11 ¼" round cake plate, oval vegetable platter

5 ½" juice pitcher with 5 ½" 12 oz. tumbler

Luncheon plate in ice blue

Oval vegetable bowl, deep salad bowl, low console bowl

MADRID

	Amber	Pink	Green	Blue		Amber	Pink	Green	Blue
Ash tray, 6" square	$225		$195		Pitcher, 8-1/2", 80 oz. ice lip	$70		$230	
Bowl, 4-3/4" cream soup	$18				Plate, 6" sherbet	$5	$4	$4	$8
Bowl, 5" sauce	$7	$7	$7	$30	Plate, 7-1/2" salad	$11	$9	$9	$20
Bowl, 7" soup	$15		$16		Plate, 8-7/8" luncheon	$9	$8	$10	$20
Bowl, 8" salad	$14		$18		Plate, 10-1/2" dinner	$45		$40	$70
Bowl, 9-3/8" lg. berry	$22	$22			Plate, 10-1/2" grill	$10		$18	
Bowl, 9-1/2" deep salad	$35				Plate, 10-1/4" relish	$15	$13	$16	
Bowl, 10" oval veg.	$15	$15	$20	$40	Plate, 11-1/4" rd. cake	$14	$10		
Bowl, 11" low console	$15	$11			Platter, 11-1/2" oval	$16	$15	$17	$25
Butter dish w/lid	$90		$100		Salt/pepper, 3-1/2" ftd.pr.	$150		$120	$170
Candlesticks, pr., 2-1/4"	$25	$25							
Cookie jar w/lid	$45	$30			Salt/pepper, 3-1/2" flat, pr.	$45		$64	
Creamer, ftd.	$9		$11	$20	Saucer	$4	$5	$5	$10
Cup	$7	$8	$9	$16	Sherbet, two styles	$8		$11	$15
Gravy boat and platter	$1500				Sugar	$8		$9	$15
Hot dish coaster	$50		$50		Sugar cover	$45		$50	$175
Hot dish coaster w/Indent	$40		$40		Tumbler, 3-7/8", 5 oz.	$15		$35	$40
Jam dish, 7"	$25		$20	$40	Tumbler, 4-1/4", 9 oz.	$15	$15	$20	$30
Jello mold, 2-1/8" T	$14				Tumbler, 5-1/2", 12 oz. 2 styles	$25		$35	$45
Pitcher, 5-1/2", 36 oz. juice	$40				Tumbler, 4", 5 oz. ftd.	$30		$40	
Pitcher, 8", sq. 60 oz.	$50	$40	$140	$165	Tumbler, 5-1/2", 10 oz. ftd.	$30		$40	
Pitcher, 8-1/2", 80 oz.	$70		$250						

Anchor Hocking Corporation, 1938-41
Colors: crystal, pink, green, red (ruby red)

Crystal dinner plate

Once not a popular pattern, *Manhattan* has found intense interest from collectors enamoured with the Art Deco movement. Originally dubbed *Ribbed,* creamers, sugars, and dessert bowls are the most abundant. Westmoreland Glass Company produced some larger pieces such as bowls and sandwich servers in a similar pink and green design in 1929.

The green seems to be the most difficult color to locate with ruby red and pink following closely behind. Pink was introduced in 1940. One of the most popular items in this pattern is the five-section relish tray with contrasting colored inserts. The round tilted pitcher is also quite popular with collectors. But of most interest seems to be the compotes, which double as Margarita glasses. Art Deco collectors are collecting sets of these to be used as cocktail glasses for this Mexican drink, thus driving up the prices quite extensively.

10 ¼" dinner plate, 8 ½" salad plate, 6" sherbet or saucer

Handled 4 ½" sauce bowl, sherbet, and 4" round ashtray

Creamer, sugar, candlestick (look-alike), and 8" vase

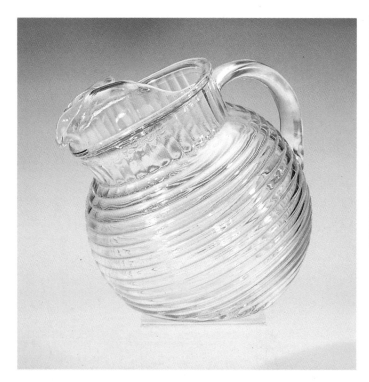

14" relish tray with four ruby inserts

80 oz. tilted pitcher

Creamer, sugar bowl, comport, footed (3-legged) candy dish

Tilted 80 oz. pitcher with footed tumblers

4 ½" sauce bowl with handles with 9 ½" open handled fruit bowl

MANHATTAN, "HORIZONTAL RIBBED,"

	Crystal	Pink		Crystal	Pink
Ashtray, 4" round	$14		Relish tray, 14", 4-part	$25	
Ashtray, 4-1/2" square	$20		Relish tray, 14" with inserts	$80	$80
Bowl, 4-1/2" sauce, handles	$9		Relish tray insert	$6	$7
Bowl, 5-3/8" berry w/handles	$20	$20	Pitcher, 24 oz.	$35	
Bowl, 5-1/4" cereal, no handles	$55	$95	Pitcher, 80 oz. tilted	$55	$75
Bowl, 7-1/2" large berry	$15		Plate, 6" sherbert or saucer	$7	$50
Bowl, 8", closed handles	$22	$25	Plate, 8-1/2 salad	$15	
Bowl, 9" salad	$25		Plate, 10-1/4" dinner	$20	$200
Bowl, 9-1/2" fruit open handle	$35	$35	Plate, 14" sandwich	$22	
Candlesticks, 4-1/2" (square) pr.	$25		Salt & pepper, 2" pr. (square)	$30	$45
Candy dish, 3 legs		$12	Saucer/sherbert plate	$7	$50
Candy dish and cover	$40		Sherbert	$10	$15
Coaster, 3-1/2"	$15		Sugar, oval	$10	$11
Comport, 5-3/4"	$35	$38	Tumbler, 10 oz. ftd.	$20	$22
Creamer, oval	$10	$11	Vase, 8"	$22	
Cup	$18	$230	Wine, 3-1/2"	$6	

Mayfair

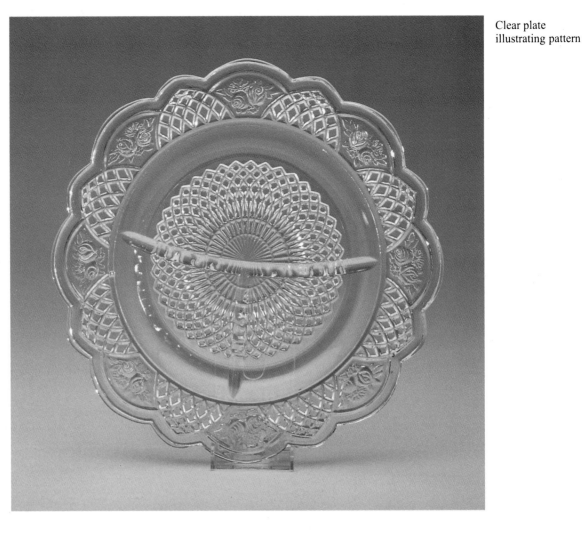

Clear plate
illustrating pattern

Federal Glass Company, 1934
Colors: amber, crystal, green

Interestingly enough, this pattern was designed by a jeweler in Columbus, Ohio. Produced under the trade pattern *Mayfair,* the patent office turned down this name since Hocking already had a *Mayfair.* At this point, Federal Glass Co., decided to abandon the pattern because the *Mayfair* molds were then redesigned into the *Rosemary* pattern. Before the patent office made its ruling, however, the pattern had been released and advertised under *Mayfair* in one issue of the *Crockery and Glass Journal,* and a small amount quickly had been sold.

The resulting design transition pieces are usually lumped in with one or the other, but they are really neither. Most certainly some collectors might consider these pieces oddities while others might find them not odd at all.

MAYFAIR,

	Amber	Crystal	Green		Amber	Crystal	Green
Bowl, 5" sauce	$9	$7	$12	Plate, 9-1/2" dinner	$14	$10	$14
Bowl, 5" cream soup	$18	$15	$18	Plate, 9-1/2" grill	$15	$9	$14
Bowl, 6" cereal	$19	$10	$20	Platter, 12" oval	$30	$20	$30
Bowl, 10" oval vegetable	$32	$20	$32	Saucer	$5	$3	$5
Creamer, ftd.	$13	$11	$16	Sugar, ftd.	$13	$11	$16
Cup	$9	$5	$9	Tumbler, 4-1/2", 9 oz.	$35	$20	$35
Plate, 6-3/4" salad	$8	$5	$9				

Hocking Glass Company, 1931-37
Colors: pink, blue, green, crystal,
yellow

9 ½" dinner plate

Most often known as *Mayfair Open Rose,* this pattern is extremely desirable to many. Much is available since it was manufactured for five years. Many wonderful pieces are available including wine glasses complete with decanter, a sweet-pea vase, beautiful sandwich server, and even whiskeys. Selected pieces were specially acid-etched to give a satin finish. Frosted salt and peppers, large and small bowls, candy jar, and cookie jar with cover were the most popular during the holiday season.

According to Hazel Weatherman, hundreds of carloads of *Mayfair* were sold in those five years of production. Plates as well as cups and saucers, however, are the more difficult pieces to find considering the large amount of this pattern sold over its production years. The original line had more than fifty items in it.

Rarest of the pieces are the three-leg, 9-inch bowl, the pair of footed salt and pepper shakers, both in pink and green, and the green or yellow footed sugars with lids. Whiskey jiggers appear in pink only.

"Frosted" or "satin" with applied paint designs including mostly flowers are also found in this pattern.

Reproduction Note: Whiskey jiggers were reproduced in 1978 and can be found in green, pink, and blue. Watch for heavier bases and indistinct mold patterns. Salt and peppers as well as the cookie jar have also been reproduced. Once again the colors are quite different when compared to the old and the molding is also quite faint when compared to the older pieces.

Dinner plate, bread and butter plate, 5 ½" cereal bowl, cup

Water tumblers with 6" pitcher

Decanter and stopper with wine goblets

8 ½" pitcher with 6 ½" footed iced tea glasses

Cookie jar w/lid, footed candy dish (no cover), and creamer

12" cake plate w/handles, Four-part square relish dish, and 10 ½" vegetable bowl

11 ¾" low flat bowl and 10" round vegetable bowl

12" deep scalloped fruit bowl

Oval vegetable bowl, oval platter, celery dish

Sandwich holder, center handle

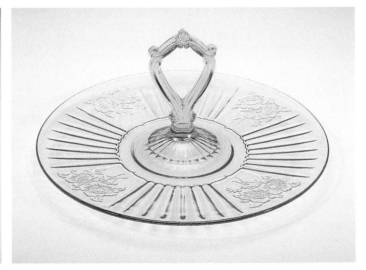

Sandwich holder in green, center handle

MAYFAIR, "OPEN ROSE,"
Hocking Glass Company, 1931-1937

	Pink	Blue	Green	Yellow
Bowl, 5" cream soup	$55			
Bowl, 5-1/2" cereal	$27	$55	$85	$85
Bowl, 7" vegetable	$30	$60	$150	$150
Bowl, 9-1/2" oval vegetable	$35	$75	$130	$145
Bowl, 10" vegetable	$28	$70		$135
Bowl, 10" same, covered	$130	$140		$1000
Bowl, 11-3/4" low flat	$60	$75	$45	$195
Bowl, 12" deep scalloped fruit	$60	$100	$45	$245
Butter dish and cover or 7" covered vegetable	$70	$300	$1300	$1300
Cake plate, 10" ftd.	$35	$75	$150	
Candy dish and cover	$60	$300	$600	$510
Celery dish, 9" divided			$195	$195
Celery dish, 10"	$45	$65	$125	$125
Celery dish, 10" divided	$250	$75		
Cookie jar and lid	$53	$295	$595	$895
Creamer, ftd.	$29	$83	$225	$225
Cup	$18	$55	$155	$155
Cup, round	$350			
Decanter and stopper, 32 oz.	$200			
Goblet, 3-3/4", 1 oz. cordial	$2000		$1000	
Goblet, 4-1/8", 2-1/2 oz.	$1000		$950	
Goblet, 4", 3 oz. cocktail	$90		$395	
Goblet, 4-1/2", 3 oz. wine	$100		$450	
Goblet, 5-1/5", 4-1/2 oz. claret	$950		$950	
Goblet, 5-3/4, 9 oz. water	$70		$495	
Goblet, 7-1/4", 9 oz. thin	$225	$195		
Pitcher, 6", 37 oz.	$60	$160	$550	$555
Pitcher, 8", 60 oz.	$60	$200	$525	$525
Pitcher, 8-1/2", 80 oz.	$110	$200	$750	$750
Plate, 5-3/4"	$14	$25	$90	$100
Plate, 6-1/2" round sherbert	$15			
Plate, 6-1/2" round, off-center indent	$25	$28	$135	$135
Plate, 8-1/2" luncheon	$30	$55	$85	$95
Plate, 9-1/2" dinner	$54	$80	$150	$165
Plate, 9-1/2" grill	$40	$55	$85	$90
Plate, 11-1/2" handled grill				$105
Plate, 12" cake w/handles	$50	$70	$40	
Platter, 12" oval, open handles	$30	$70	$165	$170
Relish, 8-3/8", 4-part	$32	$65	$165	$170
Relish, 8-3/8" non-partitioned	$225		$295	$300
Salt and pepper, flat pr.	$75	$295	$1100	$885
Sandwich server, center handle	$50	$80	$40	$135
Saucer (cup ring)	$35			$150
Saucer (see 5-3/4" plate no ringed saucer)				
Sherbert, 2-1/4" flat	$175	$125		
Sherbert, 3" ftd.	$20			
Sherbert, 4-3/4" ftd.	$80	$78	$165	$165
Sugar, ftd.	$35	$85	$210	$210
Sugar lid	$1500		$1100	$1100
Tumbler, 3-1/2", 5 oz. juice	$45	$120		
Tumbler, 4-1/4", 9 oz. water	$30	$110		
Tumbler, 4-3/4", 11 oz. water	$200	$135	$200	$210
Tumbler, 5-1/4", 13-1/2 oz. iced tea	$65	$240		
Tumbler, 3-1/4", 3 oz. ftd. juice	$85			
Tumbler, 5-1/4", 10 oz. ftd.	$45	$130		$180
Tumbler, 6-1/2", 15 oz. ftd. iced tea	$45	$250	$220	
Vase (sweet pea)	$150	$115	$295	
Whiskey, 2-1/4", 1-1/2 oz.	$70			

10 1/4" Dinner plate

Hocking Glass Company, 1933-36
Colors: pink, crystal, green, blue, red, satin

Created by Hocking in 1933, this pattern is characterized by fine points, all of which, when polished and clean, will sparkle in the light. Even our *Miss America* pageant would have a difficult time competing with the beauty of this pattern.

Complete sets are available in pink and crystal, with green very difficult to locate. Some difficult pieces to obtain are the candy dish, the large bowls (curved and straight), the butter dish, water goblets, and water pitcher. Be careful when purchasing this pattern as many time the points around the rim (in the bowls, plates, and serving pieces) are damaged. By carefully touching the points around the edges with your fingers will assure high-quality pieces with no damage.

Hocking attempted to release many of their patterns in satin finish, and *Miss America* is no exception. The large serving pieces are somewhat abundant in the pink satin finish.

Red is the color to find in this pattern. Any piece in red is a real valuable prize. Besides pink and crystal being the most produced colors, they are also the most collected. The butter dish with cover intact as well as the shakers, 8-inch and 8 ½" pitchers, and pink goblets are all very desirable pieces in this pattern.

Reproduction Note: Covered butter dishes as well as salt and peppers have been reproduced in crystal, blue, green, pin, and amber. The hobs don't have the sharp feel of the original. Pitchers and tumblers have also been reproduced, but the new tumblers have twice as thick bottoms as the originals. The handles on the old pitchers are just below a hump on the rim of the pitcher top. New ones have no hump.

Sherbet, salad plate, dinner plate, 6 ¼" cereal bowl, salt and pepper, creamer, sugar bowl

Large straight fruit bowl, large curved fruit bowl

Candy jar and
cover, comport

11 ¾" round relish plate, 8 ¾"
four-part relish dish, and cake plate

8" water pitcher and
4 ½" water glasses

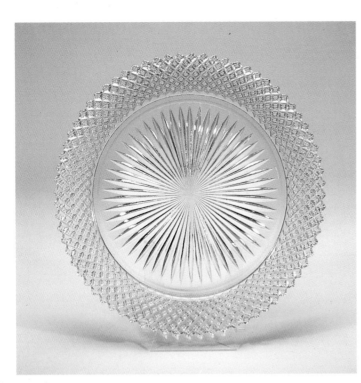

Divided grill plate, cup and saucer

Left: 10 ¼" dinner plate

Shaker, creamer, sugar bowl

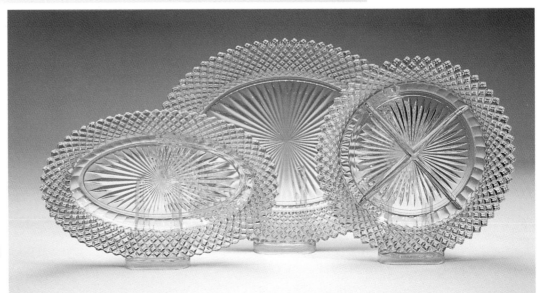

Oval vegetable bowl, oval
platter, four-part round
relish plate

5 ¾" iced tea glass with 4 ½" water glasses

8" pitcher with 5 ½" water goblet

Comport, oval vegetable bowl, large curved fruit bowl

MISS AMERICA (DIAMOND PATTERN),

	Crystal	Pink	Green		Crystal	Pink	Green
Bowl, 4-1/2" berry			$12	Pitcher, 8-1/2", 65 oz. w/ice lip	$65	$195	
Bowl, 6-1/4" cereal	$10	$25	$18	Plate, 5-3/4" sherbert	$7	$12	$7
Bowl, 8" curved in at top	$40	$85		Plate, 6-3/4"			$8
Bowl, 8-3/4" straight deep fruit	$40	$70		Plate, 8-1/2" salad	$8	$23	$10
Bowl, 10" oval vegetable	$15	$30		Plate, 10-1/4" dinner	$15	$30	
Butter dish and cover	$220	$595		Plate, 10-1/4" grill	$11	$25	
Cake plate, 12" ftd.	$26	$45		Platter, 12-1/4" oval	$15	$40	
Candy jar and cover, 11-1/2"	$70	$175		Relish, 8-3/4", 4 part	$12	$25	
Celery dish, 10-1/2" oblong	$15	$33		Relish, 11-3/4" round divided	$30		
Coaster, 5-3/4"	$20	$30		Salt and pepper, pr.	$35	$75	
Comport, 5"	$15	$30		Saucer	$4	$7	
Creamer, ftd.	$12	$25		Sherbert	$8	$15	
Cup	$12	$24	$12	Sugar	$8	$20	
Goblet, 3-3/4", 3 oz. wine	$25	$85		Tumbler, 4", 5 oz. juice	$18	$60	
Goblet, 4-3/4", 5 oz. juice	$30	$90		Tumbler, 4-1/2", 10 oz water	$15	$40	$18
Goblet, 5-1/2", 10 oz. water	$22	$45		Tumbler, 5-3/4", 14 oz. iced tea	$30	$90	
Pitcher, 8", 65 oz.	$50	$140					

Moderntone

Hazel Atlas Glass Company, 1934-37
Colors: blue, burgundy(amethyst), pink, platonite, crystal

Deep blue and purple colors are what attract many individuals to collecting this particular pattern. Fashioned in simple beauty with the concentric rings, this pattern is ageless in appearance.

Shirley Temple glass collectors will immediately recognize the blue color since this pattern was made from the blue tanks of glass used to fashion Shirley Temple novelties. While blue is the most common, burgundy or "amethyst," as most collectors call this color is very attractive as well. Later, this same mold was used to create an opaque white onto which many different bright red, blue, or yellow colors were fired. Even sprays of flowers and such similar patterns appear on this opaque white dinnerware.

Very few pieces were manufactured in pink and crystal. Mostly found is the cobalt blue. Blue and amethyst 7 ½" bowls are almost impossible to locate. The butter dish and cheese bottoms, each with metal covers, and the ashtrays are very desirable, and the prices for these pieces is quite high.

Dinner plate

Dinner plate, luncheon plate, bread and butter plate, 9 oz. tumbler, cup and saucer, sherbet

Dinner plate, 5" berry bowl, cup and saucer

MODERNTONE

	Cobalt	Amethyst
Ash tray, 7-3/4", match holder in center	$170	
Bowl, 4-3/4" cream soup	$25	$20
Bowl, 5" berry	$28	$24
Bowl, 5" cream soup, ruffled	$55	$33
Bowl, 6-1/2" cereal	$75	$75
Bowl, 7-1/2" soup	$150	$100
Bowl, 8-3/4" large berry	$50	$40
Butter dish with metal cover	$110	
Cheese dish, 7" with metal lid	$475	
Creamer	$12	$11
Cup	$12	$12
Cup (handle-less) or custard	$25	$14
Plate, 5-7/8" sherbert	$8	$6
Plate, 6-3/4" salad	$14	$10
Plate, 7-3/4" luncheon	$14	$10
Plate, 8-7/8" dinner	$18	$15
Plate, 10-1/2" sandwich	$60	$40
Platter, 11" oval	$50	$38
Platter, 12" oval	$80	$50
Salt and pepper, pr.	$50	$35
Saucer	$5	$4
Sherbert	$15	$14
Sugar	$11	$10
Sugar lid in metal	$40	
Tumbler, 5 oz.	$55	$35
Tumbler, 9 oz.	$38	$30
Tumbler, 12 oz.	$110	$90
Whiskey, 1-1/2 oz.	$50	

Salt and pepper, oval vegetable platter, custard cup, creamer, sugar bowl

Dinner plate in fired-on pink

Bud vase, tiny vase, cloverleaf bowl, candy jar and cover, straight puff bowl container (usually found with wooden top), 5 ½" crimped dessert bowl

Anchor-Hocking Glass Corporation, 1941-46
Colors: crystal with white opalescent, green with opalescent

While *Moonstone* was manufactured later than most Depression era glassware, it is still lumped into that category as it was an inexpensive, yet elegant, style glassware which appealed to millions of Americans. *Moonstone* pieces were popular wedding presents during World War II since they were reminiscent of very expensive hobnail patterns previously manufactured. White is the most commonly found, with the green being extremely rare.

Crimped flower vase (look-alike)

Sugar bowls

MOONSTONE

	Opalescent		Opalescent
Bowl, 5-1/2", berry	$20	Cup	$8
Bowl, 5-1/2", crimped dessert	$10	Goblet, 10 oz.	$25
Bowl, 6-1/2", crimped handled	$10	Heart bonbon, one handle	$15
Bowl, 7-3/4", flat	$15	Plate, 6-1/4", sherbet	$6
Bowl, 7-1/4", divided relish	$15	Plate, 8", luncheon	$15
Bowl, 9-1/2" crimped	$25	Plate, 10", sandwich	$35
Bowl, cloverleaf	$14	Puff box & cover, 4-1/4", round	$25
Candleholder, pr.	$18	Saucer (same as Sherbet plate)	$7
Candy jar & cover, 6"	$30	Sherbet, footed	$7
Cigarette jar & cover	$25	Sugar, footed	$9
Creamer	$10	Vase, 5-1/2", bud	$15

Mount Pleasant "Double Shield"

Blue and black candlestick holders

L.E. Smith Glass Company, 1930s
Colors: black, blue, green, pink

There is a great variety of shapes in this pattern. There are square and round plates, some with scalloped edges and some with scallops alternating with single and double points. Some pieces are found with gold handles and some even with gold edge trim.

There have been numerous black pieces found with sterling silver surface decorations. However, many are worn off with heavy use and can be difficult to detect.

MT. PLEASANT, "DOUBLE SHIELD,"

	Pink, Green	Amethyst, Black, Cobalt		Pink, Green	Amethyst, Black, Cobalt
Bonbon, 7", rolled-up, handled	$18	$25	Leaf, 11-1/4"		$30
Bowl, 4" opening, rose	$18	$30	Mayonnaise, 5-1/2", 3-ftd.	$18	$30
Bowl, 4-7/8", square ftd. fruit	$15	$20	Mint, 6", center handle	$16	$25
Bowl, 6", 2-handled, square	$15	$20	Plate, 7", 2-handled, scalloped	$10	$18
Bowl, 7", 3 ftd., rolled out edge	$16	$25	Plate, 8", scalloped or square	$12	$18
Bowl, 8", scalloped, 2-handled	$20	$40	Plate, 8", 2-handled	$11	$18
Bowl, 8", square, 2-handled	$19	$35	Plate, 8-1/4", square w/indent for cup		$18
Bowl, 9", scalloped, 1-3/4" deep, ftd.		$30	Plate, 9" grill		$12
Bowl, 9-1/4", square ftd. fruit	$20	$32	Plate, 10-1/2", cake, 2-handled	$16	$30
Bowl, 10", scalloped fruit		$42	Plate, 10-1/2", 1-1/4" high, cake		$40
Bowl, 10", 2-handled, turned-up edge		$32	Plate, 12", 2-handled	$20	$35
Cake plate, 10-1/2", ftd., 1-1/4" high		$40	Salt and pepper, 2 styles	$25	$42
Candlestick, single, pr.	$25	$35	Sandwich server, center-handled		$40
Candlestick, double, pr.	$30	$50	Saucer	$3	$5
Creamer	$18	$20	Sherbert, 2 styles	$10	$18
Cup (waffle-like crystal)	$5		Sugar	$20	$18
Cup	$10	$12	Tumbler, ftd.		$23
Leaf, 8"		$18	Vase, 7-1/4"		$32

Two-handled cake plates, $40-50, with handled candy plate, $30

Cake server with center handle, $45, along with two center handled bon-bon dishes, smaller, $20, larger, $25

Open handled cake plate, $35

NEW CENTURY

	Green, Crystal	Pink, Cobalt, Amethyst
Ash tray/coaster, 5-3/8"	$30	
Bowl, 4-1/2" berry	$20	
Bowl, 4-3/4" cream soup	$20	
Bowl, 8" large berry	$25	
Bowl, 9" covered casserole	$68	
Butter dish and cover	$60	
Cup	$7	$20
Creamer	$10	
Decanter and stopper	$60	
Goblet, 2-1/2 oz. wine	$30	
Goblet, 3-1/4 oz. cocktail	$25	
Pitcher, 7-3/4", 60 oz. with or without ice lip	$40	$35
Pitcher, 8", 80 oz. with or without ice lip	$40	$42
Plate, 6" sherbert	$4	
Plate, 7-1/8" breakfast	$10	
Plate, 8-1/2" salad	$10	
Plate, 10" dinner	$18	
Plate, 10" grill	$12	
Platter, 11" oval	$18	
Salt and pepper, pr.	$40	
Saucer	$5	$8
Sherbert, 3"	$9	
Sugar	$8	
Sugar cover	$15	
Tumbler, 3-1/2", 5 oz.	$18	$20
Tumbler, 3-1/2", 8 oz.	$25	
Tumbler, 4-1/4", 9 oz.	$15	$18
Tumbler, 5", 10 oz.	$20	$25
Tumbler, 5-1/4", 12 oz.	$30	$35
Tumbler, 4", 5 oz. ftd.	$20	
Tumbler, 4-7/8", 9 oz. ftd.	$25	
Whiskey, 2-1/2", 1-1/2 oz.	$20	

Hazel Atlas Glass Company, 1930
Colors: green, amethyst, crystal, black, cobalt, pink

While this is one of the more simple patterns, its serene elegance appeals to collectors, especially those interested in acquiring some breakfast dishes. Having been sold for only a brief period of time, a breakfast set placed on a wooden table with place mats and a flower centerpiece is very eye-catching.

Green is the most common color in this pattern. Very few other pieces have been found in other colors. Decanters and ash trays are the scarcer items. Some fired-on opaque colors such as red, blue, yellow, and green have been located in recent years by collectors.

8" water pitcher w/lip in green

Newport

Dinner plate

Hazel Atlas Glass Company, 1936-40
Colors: Amethyst, blue, platonite, pink

Sometimes called *Hairpin,* this pattern is very simple yet very appealing to many for its simple loop design. The rich amethyst color is quite striking in a table setting. Its rich, unique color is attracting more and more collectors. The values for all colors except the platonite are quite similar. Platonite is generally more inexpensive.

NEWPORT, "HAIRPIN"

	Cobalt	Amethyst
Bowl, 4-3/4" berry	$20	$15
Bowl, 4-3/4" cream soup	$20	$18
Bowl, 5-1/4" cereal	$40	$35
Bowl, 8-1/4" large berry	$45	$42
Cup	$14	$11
Creamer	$18	$15
Plate, 5-7/8" sherbert	$8	$6
Plate, 8-1/2" luncheon	$15	$12
Plate, 8-13/16", dinner	$35	$30
Plate, 11-3/4" sandwich	$40	$35
Platter, 11-3/4" oval	$45	$40
Salt and pepper	$50	$45
Saucer	$5	$5
Sherbert	$16	$14
Sugar	$16	$14
Tumbler, 4-1/2", 9 oz.	$45	$40

Dinner plate, berry bowl, cup and saucer, mayonnaise bowl w/round tray attached, creamer

Saucer illustrating pattern

Federal Glass Company, 1933-39
Colors: pink, amber carnival, green, crystal

This pattern often nicknamed *Bouquet and Lattice* can be collected in an array of beautiful shades. It was created as a direct outgrowth of pink tableware, which became so suddenly fashionable in the 1930s. The pink color was referred to as "Rose Glow" and the carnival color was called "Sunburst," created by spraying iridescent amber onto the pattern crystal and subsequently firing it on so well that some people might consider it carnival glass. Much of this amber carnival was shipped to the Great Northern Products Company to be used as premiums.

Later the design was reissued in *Golden Glow* as well as pink. At this later period, a water pitcher, glasses, and salt-and-pepper were added to the line. Pink and amber are the most abundant with small quantities of green and crystal being manufactured.

The pitchers, covered sugars, and salt and pepper shakers are the most collectible in this pattern as they are the most difficult to locate. So buy them when you find them.

NORMANDIE, "BOUQUET AND LATTICE"

	Amber	Pink	Iridescent
Bowl, 5" berry	$8	$9	$6
Bowl, 6-1/2" cereal	$30	$35	$9
Bowl, 8-1/2" large berry	$20	$25	$15
Bowl, 10" oval veg.	$20	$38	$18
Creamer, ftd.	$9	$12	$8
Cup	$8	$9	$6
Pitcher, 8", 80 oz.	$85	$170	
Plate, 6" sherbert	$5	$4	$3
Plate, 7-3/4" salad	$9	$11	$55
Plate, 9-1/4" luncheon	$9	$14	$15
Plate, 11" dinner	$33	$115	$15
Plate, 11" grill	$15	$20	$9
Platter, 11-3/4"	$18	$28	$12
Salt and pepper, pr.	$50	$80	
Saucer	$4	$4	$3
Sherbert	$7	$9	$8
Sugar	$8	$9	$6
Sugar lid	$100	$195	
Tumbler, 4", 5 oz. juice	$35	$75	
Tumbler, 4-1/4", 9 oz. water	$20	$55	
Tumbler, 5", 12 oz. iced tea	$40	$125	

Sherbet, cup and saucer

Large luncheon plate

Indiana Glass Company, 1930-33
Colors: yellow, green

While this pattern is placed here in this alphabetical listing, many collectors might only recognize it by another title, *Horseshoe.* Merely glancing at the intricate pattern and large round loop dominating it quickly illustrates how it earned its nickname.

The yellow is often referred to as "topaz." Quite heavy bases distinguish the pitcher, sherbets, and footed glasses while a light "airy" effect is often noticed by collectors in the bowls and plates. Its deeply etched pattern lends itself to display in windows and lighted china cabinets.

Large luncheon plate with 6 ½" berry bowl

Oval platter, 11 ½" sandwich plate, 9 ½" large berry bowl

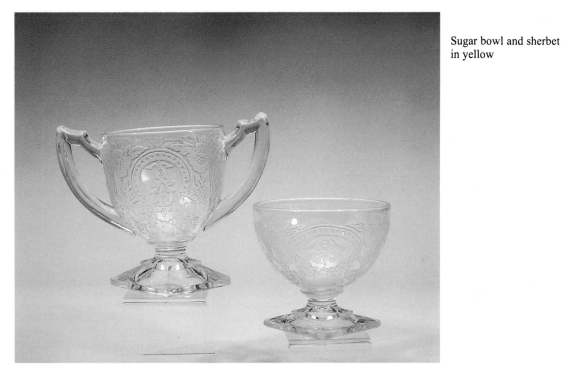

Sugar bowl and sherbet in yellow

NO. 612, "HORSESHOE,"

	Green	Yellow		Green	Yellow
Bowl, 4-1/2" berry	$30	$25	Plate, 9-3/8" luncheon	$15	$16
Bowl, 6-1/2" cereal	$30	$30	Plate, 19-3/8" grill	$125	$130
Bowl, 7-1/2" salad	$28	$28	Plate, 11-1/2" sandwich	$25	$25
Bowl, 8-1/2" vegetable	$35	$35	Platter, 10-3/4" oval	$30	$30
Bowl, 9-1/2" large berry	$45	$50	Relish, 3 part ftd.	$25	$40
Bowl, 10-1/2" oval vegetable	$25	$30	Saucer	$5	$5
Butter dish and cover	$800		Sherbert	$15	$16
Candy in metal holder motif on lid	$190		Sugar, open	$16	$17
Creamer, ftd.	$18	$20	Tumbler, 4-1/4", 9 oz.	$180	
Cup	$12	$13	Tumbler, 4-3/4", 12 oz.	$180	
Pitcher, 8-1/2", 64 oz.	$300	$340	Tumbler, 9 oz. ftd.	$30	$35
Plate, 6" sherbert	$8	$9	Tumbler, 12 oz. ftd.	$165	$180
Plate, 8-3/8" salad	$12	$12			

Old Cafe

11" plate

Hocking Glass Company, 1936-40
Colors: pink, crystal, ruby

While this pattern is quite attractively vibrant when cleaned and displayed, it is often overlooked. Its simple ray design molded in clean mold lines actually creates a pattern, which is easily assembled in pink and crystal. Many of the pieces were originally created as premiums, especially the low, flared-out mint tray and the handled oblong olive dish.

Sometimes Hocking mixed crystal and red in items such as cups and saucers and covered candy dishes. Pitchers are the most difficult to locate in this pattern.

OLD CAFE

	Crystal, Pink	Royal Ruby		Crystal, Pink	Royal Ruby
Bowl, 3-3/4" berry	$5	$7	Olive dish, 6" oblong	$8	
Bowl, 4-1/2", tab handles	$7		Pitcher, 6", 36 oz.	$85	
Bowl, 5-1/2" cereal	$20	$13	Pitcher, 80 oz.	$110	
Bowl, 6-1/2", tab handles	$25		Plate, 6" sherbert	$3	
Bowl, 9", closed handles	$14	$17	Plate, 10" dinner	$60	
Candy dish, 8" low, tab handles	$14	$17	Saucer	$3	
Candy jar, 5-1/2", crystal with ruby cover		$18	Sherbet, 3/4" low ftd.	$14	$14
Cup	$8	$10	Tumbler, 3" juice	$14	$15
Lamp	$25	$35	Tumbler, 4" water	$15	$25
			Vase, 7-1/4"	$25	$30

side view of plate

Dinner plates in assorted fired-on colors, creamer, sugar, cup, saucer, cereal bowl

**Hazel Atlas Glass Company,
1929-35
Colors: green, burgundy,
yellow, white, black**

First manufactured in green, it was made in black in 1932. By 1951, platonite or opaque white glass was used with fired-on colors. Bright green, orange, yellow, and burgundy were popular choices for people who sought the unusual in glass colors for their table settings.

OVIDE

	Black	Green	Decorated White
Bowl, 4-3/4" berry			$9
Bowl, 5-1/2" cereal			$15
Bowl, 8" large berry			$25
Candy dish and cover	$50	$25	$35
Cocktail, ftd. fruit	$6	$5	
Creamer	$7	$5	$18
Cup	$7	$4	$14
Plate, 6" sherbet		$3	$8
Plate, 8" luncheon		$4	$15
Plate, 9" dinner			$25
Platter, 11"			$25
Salt and pepper, pr.	$30	$30	$25
Saucer	$4	$3	$7
Sherbet	$7	$4	$14
Sugar, open	$7	$5	$18
Tumbler			$18

10 ¼" divided relish, illustrating pattern

Anchor Hocking Corporation, 1936-38
Colors: pink, crystal, ruby, opaque white with colored trims

Interestingly enough, this pattern was never produced in a complete table series. Always advertised as occasional pieces, this pattern was cast into many different colors and designs. Many older "vintage" collectors might remember the heart-shaped jelly dish and the 6 ½" bonbon which were produced specifically for use as premiums in oatmeal boxes.

The opaque white items are pink or green on the inside and white on the outside.

OYSTER AND PEARL

Divided relish dish and 6 ½" double handled bowl

	Crystal, Pink	Royal Ruby
Bowl, 5-1/4" heart-shaped, 1-handled	$14	$18
Bowl, 5-1/2", 1-handled	$10	$15
Bowl, 6-1/2" deep-handled	$15	$25
Bowl, 10-1/2" deep fruit	$28	$60
Candle holder, 3-1/2" pr.	$40	$60
Plate, 13-1/2" sandwich	$25	$50
Relish dish, 10-1/4" oblong, divided	$25	

Parrot

"PARROT," SYLVAN

Federal Glass Company, 1932
Colors: green, amber, crystal, blue

Parrot owes its history to the fact that one of the company's designers had just returned from an extended stay in the Bahamas when he was asked by his superiors to produce a new design pattern. All he could think of were palm trees and parrots. Thus the inspiration for this very elegant and artfully designed glass is recorded in history.

While the designer felt the pattern was fantastic, officials of Federal felt that it would not be popular since there was so much clear space, which would scratch easily. So suddenly, a decision was made to use the molds, keeping the original shape and create a new etched pattern which collectors know today as *Madrid*. As a result, its production history was so short that *Parrot* never got a chance to be advertised in company catalogs. While mostly green was created, some pieces in a light amber also were produced. The shades of green varied to quite an extent and there are some pieces which are yellowish-green, almost appearing to be a type of vaseline glass.

Green is the easiest color to collect with amber following close behind. All the other colors are quite rare.

	Green	Amber
Bowl, 5" berry	$25	$18
Bowl, 7" soup	$55	$35
Bowl, 8" large berry	$90	$80
Bowl, 10" oval vegetable	$55	$70
Butter dish and cover	$375	$1250
Creamer, ftd.	$50	$65
Cup	$40	$40
Jam dish, 7"		$35
Pitcher, 8-1/2", 80 oz.	$2850	
Plate, 5-3/4" sherbet	$35	$23
Plate, 7-1/2" salad	$40	
Plate, 9" dinner	$55	$40
Plate, 10-1/2" round grill	$40	
Plate, 10-1/2" square grill		$30
Plate, 10-1/4" square (crystal only)	$28	
Platter, 11-1/4" oblong	$52	$75
Salt and pepper, pr.	$275	
Saucer	$15	$15
Sherbet, ftd. cone	$25	$25
Sugar	$35	$40
Sugar cover	$150	$450
Tumbler, 4-1/4", 10 oz.	$140	$110
Tumbler, 5-1/2", 12 oz.	$170	$125
Tumbler, 5-3/4" ftd. heavy	$130	$110
Tumbler, 5-1/2", 10 oz. ftd. (Madrid mold)	$160	

10 ½" divided grill dinner plate with 5" berry bowl

10 ½" dinner plate

Federal Glass Company, 1933-37
Colors: amber, green, pink, crystal

First produced toward the end of 1932, in "Golden Glow" (amber) and "Springtime green," this pattern was first promoted commercially in January, 1933. Many collectors also refer to this pattern as Spoke.

Creamed soups were added in 1934 with pink and green being produced around this period of time. By 1935, the catalog listed only the amber color for sale. The 10 ½ dinner plate in amber was used as a promotional item, thus its great availability. The hexagonal cookie jar and water pitcher add to the novelty of this very intricate pattern.

Amber is the more commonly collected color simply because it is in great supply. Covered pieces, pitchers, and tumblers in any color are the most desirable; they command high prices and should be picked up when found.

Dinner plate, large berry bowl, 5" berry bowl, cup, saucer

5 ¼" footed tumblers, cup, sugar bowl, sherbet

PATRICIAN, "SPOKE"

	Amber, Crystal	Pink	Green		Amber, Crystal	Pink	Green
Bowl, 4-3/4" cream soup	$16	$18	$20	Plate, 6" sherbet	$11	$9	$9
Bowl, 5" berry	$13	$12	$12	Plate, 7-1/2" salad	$15	$15	$14
Bowl, 6" cereal	$25	$25	$28	Plate, 9" luncheon	$12	$10	$11
Bowl, 8-1/2" large berry	$50	$25	$40	Plate, 10-1/2" dinner	$7	$40	$45
Bowl, 10" oval vegetable	$35	$25	$35	Plate, 10-1/2" grill	$15	$15	$15
Butter dish and cover	$90	$230	$110	Platter, 11-1/2" oval	$30	$25	$25
Butter dish bottom	$65	$175	$75	Salt and pepper, pr.	$55	$85	$60
Butter dish top	$30	$50	$50	Saucer	$10	$10	$10
Cookie jar and cover	$85		$600	Sherbet	$13	$14	$14
Creamer, footed	$11	$12	$12	Sugar	$9	$9	$9
Cup	$9	$12	$12	Sugar cover	$60	$65	$60
Jam dish	$33	$30	$45	Tumbler, 4", 5 oz.	$35	$35	$35
Pitcher, 8", 75 oz.				Tumbler, 4-1/4", 9 oz.	$30	$30	$30
moulded handle	$120	$110	$125	Tumbler, 5-1/2", 14 oz.	$50	$40	$50
Pitcher, 8-1/4", 75 oz.,				Tumbler, 5-1/4", 8 oz. ftd.	$55		$65
applied handle	$160	$135	$150				

Peacock and Wild Rose and Peacock Reverse, Paden City

Paden City Glass Manufacturing Company, 1928-1930s
Colors: cobalt blue, green, pink

Paden City's number 300 line referred to by collectors as *Peacock and Wild Rose* has many different items in its line. *Peacock Reverse* is very similar in design as well. Pieces are found as blanks with no decorations. However, most were utilized widely by the company for etching all sorts of designs. This design is the most difficult to locate and the cups in this pattern are the rarest.

11 ¾" console bowl with deep etching, top view

Large console bowl with "Peacock Reverse" etching

Mayonnaise, liner bowl, and glass spoon

Elliptical 8 ¼" black vase

12" green vase

Larger size 6" ice tub

Large ice tub, candlestick holder,
comport

11 ¾" console bowl, blank with no pattern

"PEACOCK REVERSE"

	All Colors
Bowl, 4-7/8" square	$50
Bowl, 8-3/4" square	$120
Bowl, 8-3/4" square with handles	$125
Bowl, 11-3/4" console	$160
Candlesticks, 5-3/4" square base, pr.	$150
Candy dish, 6-1/2" square	$195
Comport, 3-1/4" high, 6-1/4" wide	$95
Comport, 4-1/4" high, 7-3/8" wide	$90
Creamer, 2-3/4" flat	$90
Cup	$90
Plate, 5-3/4" sherbet	$25
Plate, 8-1/2" luncheon	$65
Plate, 10-3/8", 2-handled	$100
Saucer	$25
Sherbet, 4-5/8" tall, 3-3/8" diameter	$75
Sherbet, 4-7/8" tall, 3-5/8" diameter	$70
Server, center-handled	$95
Sugar, 2-3/4" flat	$90
Tumbler, 4", 10 oz. flat	$100
Vase, 10"	$215

"PEACOCK & WILD ROSE"

	All Colors
Bowl, 8-1/2", flat	$130
Bowl, 8-1/2", fruit, oval, ftd.	$195
Bowl, 9-1/2", ftd.	$195
Bowl, 10-1/2", center-handled	$125
Bowl, 10-1/2" fruit	$185
Bowl, 14", console	$200
Candlestick, 5" wide, pr.	$175
Candlesticks, octagonal tops, pr.	$180
Candy dish w/cover, 6-1/2", 3 part	$175
Candy dish w/cover, 7"	$230
Candy with lid, ftd., 5-1/4" high	$175
Ice tub, 4-3/4"	$190
Ice tub, 6"	$180
Mayonnaise and liner	$100
Pitcher, 5" high	$250
Plate, cake, low foot	$165
Tumbler, 2-1/4", 3 oz.	$50
Tumbler, 3"	$60
Tumbler, 4"	$70
Tumbler, 4-3/4", ftd.	$75
Tumbler, 5-1/4", 10 oz.	$80
Vase, 12"	$315

Center handled
sandwich plate and
large console bowl

8" salad plate

Macbeth-Evans, 1930-40
Colors: pink, crystal, blue, cremax, monax

This tableware is very thin and delicate with concentric circles emanating from the center of the plates. A fine-scalloped edge further distinguishes this pattern from other Depression era glassware.

By 1936, Macbeth-Evans was producing this pattern in a monax color with cremax to follow. Some of these pieces have concentric circles and some do not. Later in 1936, the Macbeth-Evans division of Corning Glass Works experimented with many versions of *Petalware*. Three pastel bands of pink, blue and green were created. Also gold-rimmed *Petalware* was created which invariably had a floral design in bright colors created on the monax pieces.

Only four pieces of blue have been reported so far, other than the commonly found metal covered mustard. They are the 8 ¾" bowl, the footed creamer, footed sherbet, and the footed sugar bowl.

By 1940, the pattern was retired with the last pieces being primarily monax in color with no trim added.

Salad plate, sherbet plate, creamer, cup and saucer

9" berry bowl, 5 ¾" cereal bowl, 13" oval platter

Monax 12" Salver and oval 13" platter

Large close-up of pink platter

PETALWARE

	Crystal	Pink	Monax Plain	Cremax, Monax, Florette, Fired-On Decorations
Bowl, 4-1/2" cream soup	$5	$13	$12	$14
Bowl, 5-3/4" cereal	$4	$11	$8	$14
Bowl, 7" soup			$65	$75
Bowl, 9" large berry	$9	$20	$18	$35
Cup	$3	$7	$5	$10
Creamer, ftd.	$3	$8	$6	$13
Pitcher, 80 oz. (crystal decorated bands)	$30			
Plate, 6" sherbet	$2	$3	$3	$7
Plate, 8" salad	$2	$10	$4	$10
Plate, 9" dinner	$4	$18	$9	$16
Plate, 11" salver	$5	$15	$10	$18
Plate, 12" salver		$15	$20	
Platter, 13" oval	$9	$20	$15	$25
Saucer	$2	$3	$3	$4
Saucer, cream soup liner			$20	
Sherbet, 4" low ftd.			$35	
Sherbet, 4-1/2" low ftd.	$4	$10	$8	$12
Sugar, ftd.	$3	$8	$6	$10
Tidbit servers or lazy susans, several styles	$12	$15	$25	$25

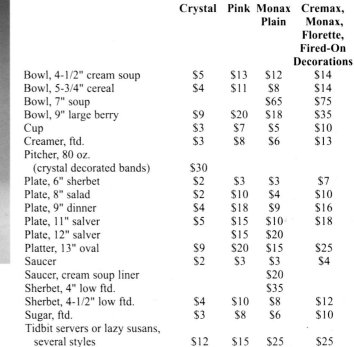

Crystal dinner plate

PRETZEL

Indiana Glass Company, 1930-70s
Colors: crystal

While company catalogs list this pattern only as No. 622, collectors have dubbed it *Pretzel* because the twisted lines looped through the plate remind one of pretzels. Still another faction of collectors refer to the pattern as *Ribbon*. They are reminded of a pressed glass pattern which goes by the same name. It is an inexpensive pattern to collect, but only a limited number of items are available. The two handled pickle dish, celery dish, and the leaf-shaped olive dish were made in huge quantities into the 1970s.

	Crystal
Bowl, 7-1/2"	$5
Bowl, 9-3/8"	$12
Celery dish, 10-1/4"	$5
Creamer	$7
Sugar	$6
Cup	$6
Saucer	$2
Olive dish (leaf shaped), 7"	$5
Pickle dish (2-handled), 8-1/2"	$6
Pickle dish (tab handled)	$7
Plate, 6"	$3
Plate, 8-3/8"	$5
Plate, 9-3/8"	$8
Plate, 11-1/2"	$12
Sherbet	$7

Hocking Glass Company, 1931-34
Colors: green, pink, yellow, satin finish

This finely-executed, mold-etched pattern is distinguished by some very interestingly shaped pieces. Of special note are the hat-shaped flower bowls, the octagonal salad bowl, and the creamer-and-sugar set. Sherbets and tumblers are of a thinner glass. Upon careful observation, collectors distinguish between the two designs on the bases of the footed items: checked and rayed.

Princess plates can be found in numerous sizes, including the grill or divided plates, which were a popular novelty of the period. Simple basic sets were first available in green, then in "topaz." Later, topaz was dropped and pink "Flamingo" was added. Certain pieces were treated with acid to produce what are referred to as "Satin Finish." This almost opaque glass was ornamented with hand-painted flower motifs.

There are no true saucers for the cups in this pattern. They are the same as the 5 ½" sherbet plates.

9 ½" dinner plate

Creamer, sugar bowl w/cover, sherbet plate, cup

Candy dish w/cover, cookie jar w/
cover, footed sherbet, creamer

8", 60 oz. pitcher with four
water glasses

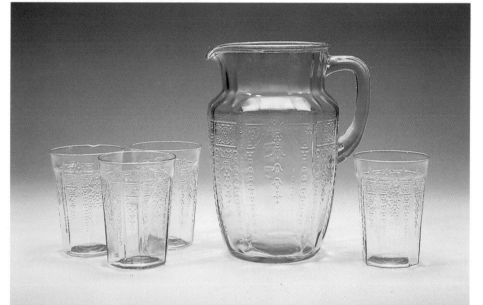

9 ½" dinner plate in pink

Divided relish plate, handled sandwich plate, and footed cake plate

Iced tea glass, sherbet, dinner plate, bread and butter plate, cup

Cookie jar and cover

6" pink pitcher with 4" water glass

Octagon salad bowl, 5" cereal bowl, butter dish w/cover, oval vegetable bowl

9" dinner plate in topaz

PRINCESS

	Green	Pink	Topaz, Apricot
Ash tray, 4-1/2"	$70	$85	$100
Bowl, 4-1/2" berry	$25	$25	$50
Bowl, 5" cereal or oatmeal	$35	$35	$32
Bowl, 9" octagonal salad	$40	$35	$140
Bowl, 9-1/2" hat-shaped	$50	$45	$140
Bowl, 10" oval vegetable	$30	$28	$65
Butter dish and cover	$150	$150	$80
Cake stand, 10"	$30	$33	

	Green	Pink	Topaz, Apricot
Candy dish and cover	$65	$70	
Coaster	$40	$70	$100
Cookie jar and cover	$60	$70	
Creamer, oval	$20	$20	$14
Cup	$12	$12	$8
Pitcher, 6", 37 oz.	$52	$65	$595
Pitcher, 7-3/8", 24 oz. ftd	$600	$500	
Pitcher, 8", 60 oz.	$55	$55	$95
Plate, 5-1/2" sherbet	$10	$10	$3
Plate, 8" salad	$15	$15	$16
Plate, 9-1/2" dinner	$26	$25	$15
Plate, 9-1/2" grill	$15	$15	$6
Plate, 10-1/4" handled sandwich	$18	$30	$175
Plate, 10-1/2" grill, closed handles	$10	$12	$6
Platter, 12" closed handles	$25	$25	$65
Relish, 7-1/2" divided	$26	$28	$100
Relish, 7-1/2" plain	$145	$195	$250
Salt and pepper, 4-1/2" pr.	$80	$80	$90
Spice shakers, 5-1/2" pr.	$40		
Saucer (same as sherbet plate)	$10	$10	$3
Sherbet, ftd.	$24	$24	$35
Sugar	$10	$12	$9
Sugar cover	$22	$18	$22
Tumbler, 3", 5 oz. juice	$35	$35	$35
Tumbler, 4", 9 oz. water	$30	$30	$30
Tumbler, 5-1/4", 13 oz. iced	$45	$35	$35
Tumbler, 4-3/4", 9 oz. sq. ftd.	$80	$80	
Tumbler, 5-1/4", 10 oz. ftd.	$35	$35	$25
Tumbler, 6-1/2", 12-1/2 oz. ftd.	$100	$100	$185
Vase, 8"	$40	$45	

Dinner plate, cup and saucer

Pyramid

Four-part handled relish tray

Indiana Glass Company, 1930s
Colors: black, pink, crystal, white (opaque), green, yellow

This pattern was essentially an accessory tableware for there are no dinner plates, no cups, etc. There are only serving pieces. Art Deco collectors have discovered this pattern; so it is quickly snapped up as it is found. In addition, the prices have escalated quite quickly due to its current popularity.

Reproduction Note: Pyramid has been reissued twice. In the 1950s, it was reissued in opaque white and topaz. In 1974, the pattern was produced in black for distribution through Tiara Home Products at home party sales.

"PYRAMID"

	Crystal	Pink	Green	Yellow
Bowl, 4-3/4" berry	$12	$20	$25	$35
Bowl, 8-1/2" master berry	$25	$35	$40	$65
Bowl, 9-1/2" oval, handled	$30	$40	$40	$60
Bowl, 9-1/2" pickle, 5-3/4" wide	$20	$35	$35	$55
Creamer	$20	$30	$30	$40
Ice tub	$75	$95	$100	$250
Pitcher	$400	$230	$250	$475
Relish tray, 4-part handled	$40	$50	$65	$75
Sugar	$20	$35	$35	$45
Tray for creamer and sugar	$30	$35	$35	$60
Tumbler, 8 oz. ftd., 2 styles	$55	$40	$45	$70
Tumbler, 11 oz. ftd.	$75	$60	$70	$95

Dinner plate

Hocking Glass Company, 1936-39
Colors: pink, crystal, green, ruby red

Queen Mary can be confused with Heisey's *Ridgeleigh,* though Heisey's pattern is marked with their familiar trademark. First introduced in pink in 1936, the ribbed design is quite elegant. A complete table service is possible to col-lect in both the pink and the crystal. There are many extra pieces including some very attractive candle holders, relish plates, and a four-section, 14" sandwich and relish plate.

Ruby red was released in the 1940s. There are two distinct types of cups to this pattern. The candy dish with cover, butter dish with cover, 9 ¾" plate, and the salt and pepper shakers in pink are the highest priced items in this pattern.

Creamer, sugar, saucer, cup, 8 ¾" berry bowl

Double branch candlesticks, butter dish w/cover

QUEEN MARY (PRISMATIC LINE), "VERTICAL RIGGED"

	Pink	Crystal		Pink	Crystal
Ash tray, 2" x3-3/4" oval	$5	$3	Creamer, ftd.	$45	$25
Ash tray, 3-1/2" round		$3	Creamer, oval	$8	$6
Bowl, 4" one handle or none	$5	$4	Cup, large	$7	$6
Bowl, 4-1/2", berry	$6	$4	Cup, small	$10	$8
Bowl, 5" berry	$15	$8	Plate, 6" and 6-5/8"	$5	$4
Bowl, 5-1/2", two handles	$6	$8	Plate, 8-3/4" salad		$6
Bowl, 6" cereal	$25	$9	Plate, 9-3/4" dinner	$65	$20
Bowl, 7" small	$12	$7	Plate, 12" sandwich	$18	$10
Bowl, 8-3/4" large berry	$16	$10	Plate, 14" serving tray	$22	$12
Butter dish or preserve and cover	$135	$25	Relish tray, 12", 3-part	$20	$10
Butter dish bottom	$25	$7	Relish tray, 14", 4-part	$20	$12
Butter dish top	$100	$20	Salt and pepper, pr.		$19
Candy dish and cover	$40	$22	Saucer/cup ring	$5	$3
Candlesticks, 4-1/2" double branch, pr.		$15	Sherbet, ftd.	$10	$8
Celery or pickle dish, 5" x10"	$25	$11	Sugar, ftd.	$40	$20
Cigarette jar, 2" x3" oval	$8	$6	Sugar, oval	$8	$5
Coaster, 3-1/2"	$8	$3	Tumbler, 3-1/2", 5 oz. juice	$10	$4
Coaster/ash tray, 4-1/4" square	$9	$5	Tumbler, 4", 9 oz. water	$15	$6
Comport, 5-3/4"	$15	$8	Tumbler, 5", 10 oz. ftd.	$80	$40

Raindrops

4" water tumblers

Federal Glass Company, 1929-32
Colors: green, crystal

Many of the pieces of this pattern have the Federal trademark, the "F" inside a shield. The characteristic inverted dots suggest its conventional name. Being one of Federal's green "Optic Designs," this simple pattern makes a nice luncheon set, especially for a summer affair.

This pattern is quite often confused with another similar pattern of Federal's, *Thumbprint*. In this pattern the designs are round bumps, not depressions. The other pattern actually has depressions in the glass. Covered sugars as well as the salt and peppers are the most difficult to collect in this pattern.

RAINDROPS, "OPTIC DESIGN"

	Green
Bowl, 4-1/2" fruit	$8
Bowl, 6" cereal	$10
Bowl, 7-1/2" berry	$45
Cup	$8
Creamer	$9
Plate, 6" sherbet	$3
Plate, 8" luncheon	$7
Salt and pepper, pr.	$375
Saucer	$3
Sherbet	$8
Sugar	$8
Sugar cover	$45
Tumbler, 3", 4 oz.	$6
Tumbler, 2-1/8", 2 oz.	$5
Tumbler, 3-7/8", 5 oz.	$8
Tumbler, 4-1/3", 9-1/2 oz.	$10
Tumbler, 5", 10 oz.	$10
Tumbler, 5-3/8", 14 oz.	$14
Whiskey, 1-7/8", 1 oz.	$8

Sherbet plate in green

Hazel Atlas Glass Company, 1930-31
Colors: green, black, crystal, pink

Produced for a very short period of time, luncheon sets with a few extra pieces are possible to collect. The creamer-and-sugar resembles those of other Hazel Atlas patterns such as *Cloverleaf* and *New Century*. Despite the seeming simplicity of the pattern, collectors quickly learn to appreciate the classic lines when displayed together in sets.

Green is the most predominant color in this pattern. As is the case of these patterns, it is difficult to find the covers for several pieces, so the covered candy dish in this pattern commands the highest price of any item.

"RIBBON"

	Green	Black
Bowl, 4" berry	$25	
Bowl, 5" cereal	$35	
Bowl, 8" large berry	$35	$40
Candy dish and cover	$40	
Creamer, ftd.	$15	
Cup	$5	
Plate, 6-1/4" sherbet	$6	
Plate, 8" luncheon	$10	$14
Salt and pepper, pr.	$35	$50
Saucer	$3	
Sherbet, ftd.	$8	
Sugar, ftd.	$15	
Tumbler, 6", 10 oz.	$40	

6" butter plate

8 ¼" luncheon plate

Hocking Glass Company, 1927-32
Colors: green, crystal

There were two different green patterns produced which have ring designs. One made in 1927, was referred to as *Circle Design.* Then in the 1929, one called simply *Ring* was produced. *Ring* is a bit different in shape with bands of four rings, while *Circle Design* has from four to eight horizontal bands, depending upon the piece.

Ring, when produced in crystal, appeared with black, yellow, and red rings. Prices are inexpensive considering the fact that collectors can find many unique extra pieces such as a decanter, a cocktail shaker, and ice bucket.

Luncheon plate, sherbet, and water tumblers

RING, "BANDED RINGS"

	Crystal	Decor., Green		Crystal	Decor., Green
Bowl, 5" berry	$4	$6	Plate, 11-1/4", sandwich	$8	$15
Bowl, 7" soup	$10	$14	Salt and pepper, pr., 3"	$30	$45
Bowl, 5-1/4", divided	$15	$35	Sandwich server, center handle	$16	$28
Bowl, 8" large berry	$8	$12	Saucer	$2	$3
Butter tub or ice tub	$25	$35	Sherbet, low (for 6-1/2" plate)	$8	$15
Cocktail shaker	$20	$28	Sherbet, 4-3/4" ftd.	$5	$9
Cup	$5	$5	Sugar, ftd.	$5	$6
Creamer, ftd.	$5	$6	Tumbler, 3", 4 oz.	$4	$6
Decanter and stopper	$25	$43	Tumbler, 3-1/2", 5 oz.	$5	$7
Goblet, 7-1/4", 9 oz.	$10	$15	Tumbler, 4", 8 oz., old fashion	$15	$18
Goblet, 3-3/4", 3-1/2" oz. cocktail	$11	$20	Tumbler, 4-1/4", 9 oz.	$5	$10
Goblet, 4-1/2", 3-1/2 oz. wine	$13	$20	Tumbler, 4-3/4", 10 oz.	$8	
Ice bucket	$20	$35	Tumbler, 5-1/8", 12 oz.	$10	$12
Pitcher, 8" 60 oz.	$18	$25	Tumbler, 3-1/2" ftd. juice	$10	$12
Pitcher, 8-1/2", 80 oz.	$20	$35	Tumbler, 5-1/2" ftd. water	$7	$12
Plate, 6-1/4" sherbet	$3	$3	Tumbler, 6-1/2" ftd. iced tea	$9	$20
Plate, 6-1/2", off-center ring	$6	$7	Vase, 8"	$20	$40
Plate, 8" luncheon	$3	$5	Whiskey, 2", 1-1/2" oz.	$6	$10

Green footed sherbet   Amber 6 ½" plate

Colors: green

Beginning collectors often confused this pattern with *Cameo,* due to its close similarities. Check for the rose inside the cameo and this pattern is easily recognized. Unfortunately, this very beautiful pattern was only produced in a limited number of pieces.

Federal Glass Company, 1935-36
Colors: amber, pink, green, crystal

Often dubbed *Dutch Rose* by collectors, this very elegant pattern produced from the short-lived *Mayfair* molds was offered in simple four-piece table services in "Golden Glow," its most available color even today. Very little is found in pink, green, and crystal. The sugar bowl is without a lid or handles and resembles a sherbet. Interesting enough, the pattern around the base of the cup also varies somewhat from piece to piece.

ROSE CAMEO

	Green
Bowl, 4-1/2" berry	$12
Bowl, 5" cereal	$18
Bowl, 6" straight sides	$25
Plate, 7" salad	$14
Sherbet	$14
Tumbler, 5" ftd. (2 styles)	$25

ROSEMARY, "DUTCH ROSE"

	Amber	Green	Pink
Bowl, 5" berry	$8	$10	$10
Bowl, 5" cream soup	$18	$25	$30
Bowl, 6" cereal	$30	$25	$40
Bowl, 10" oval vegetable	$17	$30	$40
Creamer, ftd.	$10	$14	$20
Cup	$6	$10	$11
Plate, 6-3/4" salad	$6	$9	$10
Plate, dinner	$9	$14	$20
Plate, grill	$8	$15	$22
Platter, 12" oval	$17	$22	$32
Saucer	$5	$5	$6
Sugar, ftd.	$10	$14	$18
Tumbler, 4-1/4", 9 oz.	$35	$35	$60

Roulette

8 ½" luncheon plate

Hocking Glass Company, 1936-38
Colors: green, pink, crystal

While the inspiration for this pattern appears to have come from the roulette wheel, it is a "Winning Pattern" as promoted by Hocking in one of their early glass advertising brochures. It was a promotional line and made in green luncheon sets only in 1936.

While there is a pitcher, tumblers, and a fruit bowl; there is no creamer-and-sugar. A limited amount of pink was made towards the end of the manufacturing period. The light green color along with the simplistic design appeals to an ever-increasing number of Depression glass collectors.

ROULETTE, "MANY WINDOWS"

	Crystal	Pink, Green
Bowl, 9" fruit	$10	$18
Cup	$36	$7
Pitcher, 8", 65 oz.	$40	$45
Plate, 6" sherbet	$4	$5
Plate, 8-1/2" luncheon	$5	$6
Plate, 12" sandwich	$11	$14
Saucer	$2	$4
Sherbet	$4	$6
Tumbler, 3-1/4", 5 oz. juice	$8	$25
Tumbler, 3-1/4", 7-1/2 oz. old fashioned	$25	$50
Tumbler, 4-1/8", 9 oz. water	$19	$35
Tumbler, 5-1/8", 12 oz. iced tea	$20	$35
Tumbler, 5-1/2", 10 oz. ftd.	$20	$35
Whiskey, 2-1/2", 1-1/2 oz.	$15	$20

9" Fruit bowl

Sandwich plate, luncheon plate, sherbet plate, cup, saucer, sherbet, 5 ½" footed tumbler

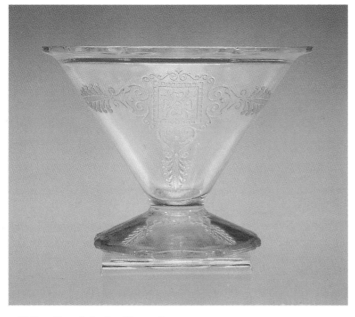

Yellow footed sherbet illustrating pattern

Dinner plate in pink

Colors: yellow

While very simple in design and shape, this very limited pattern does appeal to collectors who often mix this design with other similar patterns.

Only six different pieces have been located in this pattern. To this date, the manufacturer is unknown.

Hazel Atlas Glass Company, 1934-41
Colors: pink, green, dark blue, crystal, burgundy

This intricate lacey pattern was extremely popular when first released in 1934 and remains just as popular with collectors today. The colors changed over the years in an effort to appeal to even more collectors. Different models replaced the pitcher, console bowl, and candlesticks as the years wore on, but the other pieces remained quite standard.

In 1936, dark blue was instantly popular when used in the Shirley Temple pieces. Promotional in nature, they were cherished by Americans who revered this very famous child star. But when officials found themselves left with tanks of molten blue glass after the popularity of this glass faded, there was panic. But this panic was short-lived as the *Royal Lace* skeleton molds were quickly revived in this very dark blue, almost cobalt color.

Following this dark blue was a purple color with pieces such as the cookie jar and ice cream dishes receiving this very new tone. But this color never did catch on, especially in this period when colored glassware was declining in popularity, and the issue was very limited in run. The crystal color, however, remained a staple item with Sears, Roebuck until 1941, a long run of popularity.

The covers for many of the items were broken or lost over the years. As a result, they are more scarce and more costly than their corresponding bowls.

ROXANA

	Yellow	White
Bowl, 4-1/2"x2-3/8"	$12	$15
Bowl, 5" berry	$11	
Bowl, 6" cereal	$18	
Plate, 5-1/2"	$9	
Plate, 6" sherbet	$8	
Sherbet, ftd.	$14	
Tumbler, 4-1/4", 9 oz.	$20	

Cup, saucer, dinner plate, sugar bowl, creamer

Center left: Cup, saucer, creamer, sugar bowl

Center right: 10" round berry bowl, oval platter, cream soup bowl, three-legged, footed rolled edge console bowl

Bottom: Two styles of 8" pitchers with 9 oz. tumblers

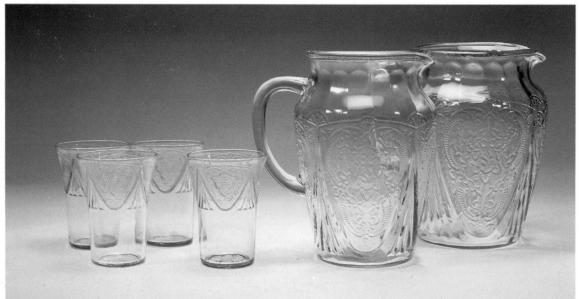

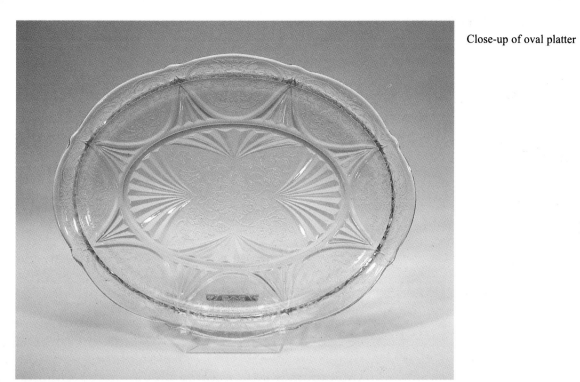

Close-up of oval platter

Dinner plate in green

Butter dish with cover

Sugar bowl and creamer

Dinner plate, salad plate, cup, saucer

Straight sides, 48 oz. pitcher with 9 oz. water tumblers

Dinner plate in blue

Cup, saucer, dinner plate, cream soup bowl, water tumbler

10" round berry bowl

Butter dish with cover

Salt and pepper shakers

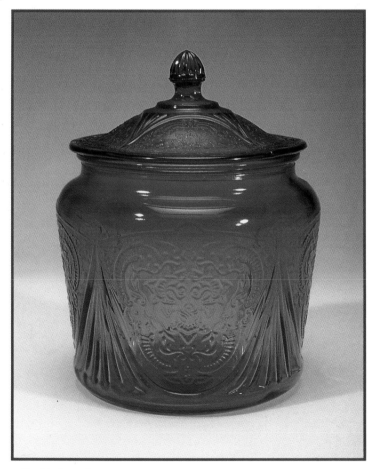

Cookie jar and cover

ROYAL LACE

	Crystal	Pink	Green	Blue
Bowl, 4-3/4" cream soup	$14	$25	$32	$45
Bowl, 5" berry	$15	$35	$40	$55
Bowl, 10" round berry	$25	$30	$35	$70
Bowl, 10", 3-legged straight edge	$30	$55	$75	$90
Bowl, 10", 3-legged rolled edge	$240	$95	$100	$425
Bowl, 10", 3-legged ruffled edge	$45	$75	$95	$495
Bowl, 11" oval vegetable	$25	$35	$40	$65
Butter dish and cover	$80	$200	$300	$700
Candlestick, straight edge pr.	$35	$100	$110	$200
Candlestick, rolled edge pr.	$65	$110	$140	$230
Candlestick ruffled edge pr.	$40	$110	$115	$250
Cookie jar and cover	$35	$90	$90	$465
Cream, ftd.	$12	$20	$25	$55
Cup	$7	$15	$20	$35
Pitcher, 48 oz., straight sides	$50	$110	$120	$170
Pitcher, 64 oz., 8" w/o/l	$45	$80	$120	$245
Pitcher, 8", 68 oz., w/lip	$50	$95		$265
Pitcher, 8", 86 oz., w/o/l	$50	$130	$200	$325
Pitcher, 8-1/2", 96 oz., w/lip	$65	$110	$160	$395
Plate, 6", sherbet	$5	$8	$10	$12
Plate, 8-1/2" luncheon	$8	$15	$16	$35
Plate, 9-7/8" dinner	$16	$30	$35	$43
Plate, 9-7/8" grill	$11	$22	$28	$35
Platter, 13" oval	$20	$40	$45	$55
Salt and pepper, pr.	$42	$65	$125	$275
Saucer	$5	$7	$9	$13
Sherbet, ftd.	$18	$18	$25	$45
Sherbet in metal holder	$4			$35
Sugar	$9	$15	$22	$25
Sugar lid	$20	$50	$55	$150
Tumbler, 3-1/2", 5 oz.	$20	$35	$35	$60
Tumbler, 4-1/8", 9 oz.	$15	$25	$35	$50
Tumbler, 4-7/8", 10 oz.	$35	$75	$70	$130
Tumbler, 5-3/8", 12 oz.	$35	$65	$60	$120

Dinner plate

Anchor Hocking Glass Company, 1939-
Colors: ruby

Hocking's first *Royal Ruby* was made in 1939, featuring round plates in dinner sets. Many accessory pieces were sold as well. Since this color was so very popular, pieces of other patterns were produced in this ruby color, including *Oysters and Pearls, Old Café,* and *Coronation*. Often combined with crystal, these pieces were extremely striking.

In 1949, the square-shaped plates were introduced and another wave of popularity ensued as Americans rushed out to purchase *Royal Ruby*. These newer pieces most often contained a center ribbed design. Roly-Poly type tumblers were introduced at this particular point as well. Frequently, footed items with crystal bases are found in this pattern.

Cup, saucer, dinner plate, 4" berry bowl, low soup bowl, low footed sherbet, stemmed sherbet

10" fruit bowl, large salad or popcorn bowl, bulbous vase

Crystal jam jar with royal ruby top, two styles of creamers and sugar bowls

Various sorts of ruby bowls including coronation pattern

Assortment of glasses including ribbed, old café, gold rimmed tumbler, and footed wine goblet

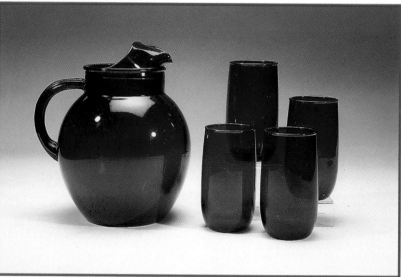

Large ice-lipped pitcher with 6" tumblers

ROYAL RUBY

	Royal Ruby		Royal Ruby
Bonbon, 6-1/2"	$10	Creamer, ftd.	$10
Bowl, 3-3/4" berry (Old Cafe)	$8	Cup (Coronation)	$7
Bowl, 4-1/2", handled (Coronation)	$7	Cup (Old Cafe)	$9
Bowl, 4-7/8", smooth (Sandwich)	$14	Cup, round	$6
Bowl, 5-1/4" heart-shaped,		Goblet, ball stem	$10
1-handled (Oys & Prl)	$18	Jewel box, 4-1/4", crys. w/Ruby cov.	$14
Bowl, 5-1/4", scalloped (Sandwich)	$20	Lamp (Old Cafe)	$35
Bowl, 5-1/2" cereal (Old Cafe)	$15	Marmalade, 5-1/8", crys. w/Ruby cov.	$8
Bowl, 5-1/2", 1-handled (Oys & Prl)	$15	Plate, 8-1/2", luncheon (Coronation)	$10
Bowl, 6-1/2" deep-handled (Oys & Prl)	$25	Plate, 9-1/8", dinner, round	$11
Bowl, 6-1/2", handled (Coronation)	$12	Plate, 13-1/2" sandwich (Oys & Prl)	$60
Bowl, 6-1/2", scalloped (Sandwich)	$30	Puff box, 4-5/8", crys. w/Ruby cov.	$9
Bowl, 8", handled (Coronation)	$15	Relish tray insert (Manhattan)	$4
Bowl, 8", scalloped (Sandwich)	$40	Saucer, round	$3
Bowl, 9", closed handles (Old Cafe)	$16	Sherbet, low ftd. (Old Cafe)	$12
Bowl, 10-1/2" deep fruit (Oys & Prl)	$65	Sugar, ftd.	$10
Candle holder, 3-1/2" pr. (Oys & Prl)	$60	Sugar, lid	$11
Candle holder, 4-1/2" pr. (Queen Mary)	$80	Tray, 6" x 4-1/2"	$14
Candy dish, 8" mint, low (Old Cafe)	$18	Tumbler, 3" juice (Old Cafe)	$15
Candy jar, 5-1/2", crys.		Tumbler, 4" water (Old Cafe)	$20
w/Ruby cov. (Old Cafe)	$18	Vase, 7-1/4" (Old Cafe)	$25
Cigarette box/card holder,		Vase, 9", two styles	$20
6-1/8" x 4" crys. w/Ruby top	$68		

"S" Pattern

8 ¼" luncheon plate

Macbeth-Evans Glass Company, 1930-32
Colors: pink, topaz, crystal, green, blue, red, yellow

Listed by Macbeth and noted by the *Crockery and Glass Journal* as the *S Pattern,* its trade-name has stayed the same. First produced in "Rose Pink," it was also sold in topaz and crystal. Most often *S Pattern* in crystal was produced with a gold band, platinum ring, and a blue band. Very little of it surfaces today since comparatively little was produced.

"S" PATTERN, "STIPPLED ROSE BAND"

	Crystal	Yellow, Amber, Crystal W/trims
Bowl, 5-1/2" cereal	$6	$8
Bowl, 8-1/2" large berry	$11	$16
Creamer, thick or thin	$6	$7
Cup, thick or thin	$4	$5
Pitcher, 80 oz. (like "Dogwood") (green or pink $550)	$55	$120
Pitcher, 80 oz. (like "American Sweetheart")	$80	
Plate, 6" sherbet (Monax $8)	$3	$3
Plate, 8-1/4" luncheon	$5	$5
Plate, 9-1/4" dinner		$10
Plate, grill	$8	$9
Plate, 11-3/4" heavy cake	$50	$60
Plate, 13" heavy cake	$70	$80
Saucer	$2	$3
Sherbet, low ftd.	$5	$7
Sugar, thick and thin	$6	$8
Tumbler, 3-1/2", 5 oz.	$8	$10
Tumbler, 4", 9 oz. (green or pink $50)	$8	$10
Tumbler, 4-3/4", 10 oz.	$10	$10
Tumbler, 5", 12 oz.	$12	$20

Sherbet plate, cup 80 oz. pitcher, 4" water tumbler

Sandwich

Amber sandwich plate illustrating pattern

Anchor Hocking Glass Company, 1939-50
Indiana Glass Company, 1920-39
Duncan Miller Glass Company, 1930-
Westmoreland Glass Company, 1930-1961
Colors: crystal, pink, green, ruby, white, amber

While all of the above manufacturers produced this pattern, it is being amassed together under this particular heading. *Sandwich* is a confusing pattern as to the manufacturer and the date of production, but it is collected in a myriad of different pieces including candlesticks, cookie jars, and elegant creamer-and-sugar sets with tray.

Hocking first issued this pattern in 1939-40, in green and ruby red. Later in the 1940s, a full line of crystal was manufactured. The 1950s brought pieces in green and a limited number of opaque white items.

Rarities include the small plate liner for the crystal custard; the pitchers, particularly the green ones; the butter dish; cookie jar and cover; and bowls in green.

Reproduction Note: This pattern is still being produced today. Thus it is one of the more confusing patterns to collect. Items are still being sold though home party sales as well.

SANDWICH

	Amber, Crystal	Teal, Blue	Red	Pink, Green
Ash trays (club, spade, heart, diamond shapes, ea.)	$4			
Basket, 10" high	$35			
Bowl, 4-1/4" berry	$4			
Bowl, 6"	$4			
Bowl, 6", hexagonal	$5	$14		
Bowl, 8-1/2"	$12			
Bowl, 9" console	$16			$50
Bowl, 11-1/2" console	$20			$50
Butter dish and cover, domed	$25	$155		
Candlesticks, 3-1/2" pr.	$16			$45
Candlesticks, 7" pr.	$30			
Creamer	$10		$45	
Celery, 10-1/2"	$16			
Creamer and sugar on diamond shaped tray	$16	$32		
Cruet, 6-1/2 oz. and stopper	$26	$140		$175
Cup	$4	$9	$28	
Decanter and stopper	$22		$80	$120
Goblet, 9 oz.	$15		$50	

	Amber, Crystal	Teal, Blue	Red	Pink, Green
Mayonnaise, ftd.	$13			$30
Pitcher, 68 oz.	$25		$140	
Plate, 6" sherbet	$3	$7		
Plate, 7" bread and butter	$4			
Plate, 8" oval, indent for cup	$6	$12		
Plate, 8-3/8" luncheon	$5		$20	
Plate, 10-1/2" dinner	$8			$20
Plate, 13" sandwich	$14	$24	$38	$28
Puff box	$16			
Salt and pepper pr.	$18			
Sandwich server, center	$18		$45	$30
Saucer	$3	$5	$8	
Sherbet, 3-1/4"	$7	$12		
Sugar, large	$10		$45	
Sugar lid for large size	$13			
Tumbler, 3 oz. ftd. cocktail	$8			
Tumbler, 8 oz. ftd. water	$9			
Tumbler, 12 oz. ftd., iced tea	$10			
Wine, 3", 4 oz.	$8		$14	$30

Sharon "Cabbage Rose"

Federal Glass Company, 1935-39
Colors: pink, amber, green, crystal

While *Sharon* is the official name for this pattern, countless collectors refer to it as *Cabbage Rose.* It was made from Federal's new "chipped mold process," a method of production devised after the mold-etched technique used earlier.

Since the footed tumblers were not part of the original set, they are relatively difficult to find today. A cheese dish and cover appeared in only one catalog, and was marketed to cheese companies to be used as a promotional item. The sugar bowl was sold with or without the cover. Watch for the two styles of pitcher: plain and ice-lipped.

Rarities are the covered cheese, salt and pepper shakers, the covered butter dish, and green footed 6 ½" tumblers.

Reproduction Note: Shakers, covered butter, cheese dishes, candy dishes, sugars, and creamers have been reproduced. All of them are crudely molded with the leaves and flowers not molded very well. The glass is generally thicker along with colors quite untrue to the original shades manufactured.

9 ½" dinner plate

Dinner plate, bread and butter plate, creamer, cream soup bowl

Large fruit bowl, low sherbet, and dinner plate

Oval platter, bread and butter plate, sugar bowl

SHARON, "CABBAGE ROSE"

	Amber	Pink	Green
Bowl, 5" berry	$9	$13	$16
Bow, 5" cream soup	$28	$48	$55
Bowl, 6" cereal	$22	$28	$28
Bowl, 7-3/4" flat soup, 1-7/8" deep	$55	$60	
Bowl, 8-1/2" large berry	$6	$35	$35
Bowl, 9-1/2" oval vegetable	$20	$35	$35
Bowl, 10-1/2" fruit	$21	$40	$45
Butter dish and cover	$48	$55	$90
Cake plate, 11-1/2" ftd.	$30	$45	$70
Candy jar and cover	$50	$50	$170
Cheese dish and cover	$200	$1000	
Creamer, ftd.	$15	$20	$25
Cup	$10	$15	$20
Jam dish, 7-1/2"	$45	$230	$45
Pitcher, 80 oz. with ice lip	$50	$180	$475
Pitcher, 80 oz. without ice lip	$150	$185	$475
Plate, 6" bread and butter	$5	$8	$8
Plate, 7-1/2" salad	$15	$25	$25
Plate, 9-1/2" dinner	$11	$20	$25
Platter, 12-1/2" oval	$20	$30	$35
Salt and pepper, pr.	$40	$50	$70
Saucer	$7	$12	$12
Sherbet, ftd.	$15	$18	$40
Sugar	$9	$14	$15
Sugar lid	$22	$33	$40
Tumbler, 4-1/8", 9 oz. thick	$30	$50	$85
Tumbler, 4-1/8", 9 oz. thin	$30	$50	$85
Tumbler, 5-1/4", 12 oz. thin	$60	$55	$110
Tumbler, 5-1/4", 12 oz. thick	$70	$90	$98
Tumbler, 6-1/2", 15 oz. ftd.	$130	$60	

7 ½" salad plate

Sierra

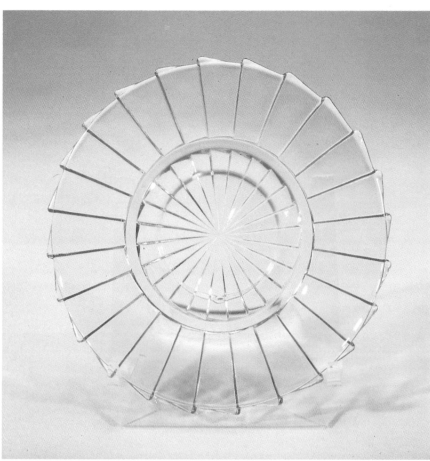

**Jeannette Glass Company, 1931-32
Colors: pink, green**

Formerly referred to as *Pinwheel,* this pattern was relatively short-lived. However, its jagged pinwheel edges and Art Deco appearance have raised its collectibility to a very high status. Its short production history was due to the discovery that the serrated edges chipped easily.

Among the most difficult pieces to find are the pitchers, tumblers, and covered butter dishes. All collectors covet the combination Adam-Sierra design butter dish when they see it.

9" dinner plate

Sugar bowl w/cover, creamer, cup, saucer, pitcher

Butter dish and cover

9" dinner plate

SIERRA, "PINWHEEL"

	Pink	Green
Bowl, 5-1/2" cereal	$18	$20
Bowl, 8-1/2" large berry	$35	$35
Bowl, 9-1/4" oval vegetable	$60	$130
Butter dish and cover	$70	$95
Creamer	$20	$25
Cup	$14	$15
Pitcher, 6-1/2", 32 oz.	$100	$140
Plate, 9" dinner	$25	$26
Platter, 11" oval	$45	$53
Salt and pepper, pr.	$50	$60
Saucer	$8	$9
Serving tray, 10-1/4", 2 handles	$15	$18
Sugar	$20	$26
Sugar cover	$16	$16
Tumbler, 4-1/2", 9 oz. ftd.	$75	$90

Footed tumbler, cup, saucer, dinner plate, 5 ½" cereal bowl

Covered sugar, creamer, oval platter, and 8 ½" large berry bowl

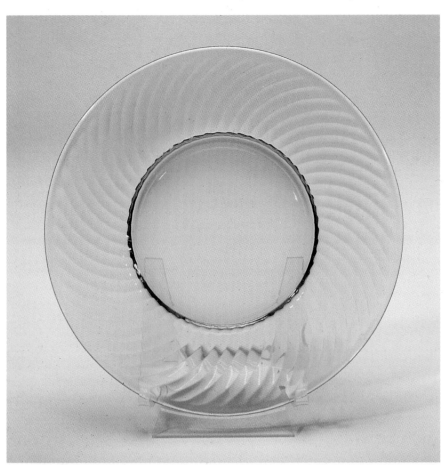

8" Luncheon plate

Hocking Glass Company, 1928-1929
Colors: green, crystal

Often a confusing pattern, collectors need to take note of the direction and shape of the swirl. Once seen, *Spiral* becomes much easier to identify. It is one of the oldest patterns to be classified under the category of Depression glass. It was made in both dinner and luncheon sets.

The syrup pitcher, a one-handled mixing bowl with spout, and the sandwich server with central handle are all interesting pieces, which add an interesting dimension to this pattern. The pitcher and tumblers are of a thinner glass than the other pieces of tableware.

It is one of the easiest patterns for beginning collectors to find since it is readily available and very low in cost.

Cup, saucer, salad plates, sherbet plate, 4 ¾" berry bowl

Sugar bowl, creamer, oval platter, preserve jar w/cover (hole for spoon) candy jar w/cover (no hole for spoon)

Large footed tumblers with 8" water pitcher

Large water tumblers
with 8" water pitcher

Bulbous style water pitcher
with 4" water tumblers

SPIRAL

	Green		Green
Bowl, 4-3/4" berry	$5	Preserve and cover	$34
Bowl, 7" mixing	$10	Salt and pepper, pr.	$45
Bowl, 8" large berry	$14	Sandwich server, center handle	$25
Creamer, flat or ftd.	$8	Saucer	$3
Cup	$5	Sherbet	$5
Ice or butter tub	$30	Sugar, flat or ftd.	$8
Pitcher, 7-5/8", 58 oz.	$30	Tumbler, 3", 5 oz. juice	$5
Plate, 6" sherbet	$2	Tumbler, 5", 9 oz. water	$8
Plate, 8" luncheon	$4	Tumbler, 5-7/8" ftd.	$15
Platter, 12"	$35	Vase, 5-3/4", ftd.	$65

Strawberry

Pink sherbet illustrating pattern

U.S. Glass Company, 1928-31
Colors: green, pink, carnival amber, crystal

While very heavy in nature, this pattern is deeply etched and easily recognized as strawberries with leaves. Made in luncheon sets, it is popular with nature lovers.

Pitchers and covered butter dishes are the most difficult to locate. The butter dish covers have the design motif, but the dishes themselves have only a center rayed design with no berries.

STRAWBERRY

	Crystal, Iridescent	Pink, Green		Crystal, Iridescent	Pink, Green
Bowl, 4" berry	$7	$10	Olive dish, 5" one-handled	$10	$20
Bowl, 6-1/4", 2" deep	$60	$100	Pickle dish, 8-1/4" oval	$9	$20
Bowl, 6-1/2" deep salad	$15	$20	Pitcher, 7-3/4"	$180	$165
Bowl, 7-1/2" deep berry	$20	$30	Plate, 6" sherbet	$8	$8
Butter dish and cover	$140	$165	Plate, 7-1/2" salad	$12	$18
Butter dish bottom	$80	$90	Sherbet	$7	$9
Butter dish top	$60	$60	Sugar, small open	$12	$20
Comport, 5-3/4"	$14	$25	Sugar large	$22	$35
Creamer, small	$14	$20	Sugar cover	$38	$60
Creamer, 4-5/8" large	$25	$40	Tumbler, 3-5/8", 8 oz.	$25	$40

Sunflower

9" dinner plate

Jeannette Glass Company, 1929-35
Colors: pink, green, delphite

While countless cake plates are discovered in this very elegant etching, collectors quickly become surprised when they come across other pieces such as dinner plates, cups, tumblers, and even ash trays. The cake plate's fame is a result of it being a promotional item for "Big Jo" flour.

The rarest piece is the 7-inch trivet or hot plate with three legs and a raised edge. Obviously, the cake plate is the most commonly found item.

SUNFLOWER

	Pink	Green
Ash Tray, 5", center design only	$10	$15
Cake Plate, 10", 3 legs	$18	$15
Creamer (opaque $85)	$18	$20
Cup (opaque $75)	$12	$15
Plate, 9" dinner	$20	$25
Saucer	$9	$10
Sugar (opaque $85)	$18	$20
Tumbler, 4-3/4", 8 oz. ftd.	$35	$40
Trivet, 7", 3 legs, turned up edge	$350	$360

Footed tumbler, dinner plate, cup, saucer, creamer, sugar bowl

Footed cake plates so very popular as promotional items

Assortment of tumblers including ring, tulip, and other floral patterns

Misc. glass companies, 1930s-50s
Colors: crystal with fired-on designs

As early as 1933, Kraft Cheese Company commenced to market cheese spreads in reusable glass tumblers. Produced in a five-ounce size, these tumblers had a smooth beverage lip and a permanent fired-on color decoration. Designs were tested and changed according to consumer demand. Hazel Atlas Glass Company produced many of these hand-decorated containers, using close to 300 employees, who worked around the clock to keep up with the demand. Very quickly, a silk screen process was developed to speed up the manufacturing process. During the War years (1941-45), *Swanky Swigs* were discontinued. They reappeared once again in 1947 being produced until 1958. Great varieties of different patterns and sizes are available.

SWANKY SWIGS

Band, Black, 3-3/8"	$3
Band, Black, 4-3/4"	$5
Carnival, Blue, Red	$6
Checkerboard, Green, 3-1/2"	$28
Circle & Dot, Blue, 4-3/4"	$9
Dot, Black, 4-3/4"	$8
Star, Blue, Red, Green, Black, 3-1/2"	$4
Tulip, Blue, Red, 4-1/2"	$18
Tulip, Dk.Blue,Lt.Blue, 3-3/4"	$4

Bottom of large bowl illustrating pattern

Jeannette Glass Company, 1937-38
Colors: pink, opaque blue, ultramarine blue, amber,
delphite

Ultramarine blue was the first color produced in this very elegant pattern. Later released in pink, collectors quickly discover the very different shade of pink quite unlike any other of the period.

There is a butter dish, a large tall flower vase, and even double candlesticks. Thus there are many different pieces to amass, producing an interesting table arrangement. *Swirl* can be a difficult pattern to collect, especially in the pink and opaque blue. Watch for the characteristic border swirls and circles concentric from the center of this very collectible pattern.

Very little delphite was made. Collectors who wish to collect the butter dish and the covered candy dish will quickly realize that these are the rarest items in this pattern. Blue and amber in any piece are very desirable as well.

Cup, sugar bowl, double branch candleholder, 9" berry bowl

Footed console bowl with footed berry bowl

SWIRL

	Pink	Ultramarine		Pink	Ultramarine
Bowl, 4-7/8" & 5-1/4" berry	$12	$18	Plate, 8" salad	$10	$15
Bowl, 9" salad	$20	$30	Plate, 9-1/4" dinner	$15	$20
Bowl, 9" salad, rimmed	$20	$30	Plate, 12-1/2" sandwich	$20	$35
Bowl, 10" ftd., closed handles	$30	$35	Salt and pepper, pr.		$45
Bowl, 10-1/2" ftd. console	$20	$30	Saucer	$4	$5
Butter dish	$200	$290	Sherbet, low ftd.	$14	$25
Candle holders, double branch pr.	$45	$55	Soup, tab handles (lug)	$30	$35
Candy dish, open, 3 legs	$14	$20	Sugar, ftd.	$10	$16
Candy dish with cover	$120	$185	Tumbler, 4", 9 oz.	$30	$40
Coaster, 1" x 3-1/4"	$10	$15	Tumbler, 4-5/8", 9 oz.	$25	
Creamer, ftd.	$10	$16	Tumbler, 5-1/8", 13 oz.	$60	$130
Cup	$10	$16	Tumbler, 9 oz.ftd.	$25	$50
Pitcher, 48 oz.ftd.		$1900	Vase, 6-1/2" ftd., ruffled	$20	
Plate, 6-1/2" sherbet	$5	$8	Vase, 8-1/2" ftd., two styles		$20
Plate, 7-1/4"	$9	$15			

Tea Room

Creamer and
sugar bowl

Indiana Glass Company, 1927-31
Colors: pink, green, amber, crystal

This gigantic line was released in *Tea Room and Fountain Service* by Indiana Glass Company in 1926. It was designed for use in restaurants and soda-fountains of the period, and is very heavy and sturdy in design. Once found to

be merely an interesting pattern, *Tea Room* has become immensely popular with collectors today. Its stylistic shape and appearance fits the tastes of Art Deco collectors who regularly snatched up every piece they come across.

Any piece in amber and the pitcher in crystal will bring quite a high price as they are quite rare.

TEA ROOM

	Green	Pink		Green	Pink
Bowl, finger	$60	$45	Salt and pepper, pr.	$55	$50
Bowl, 7-1/2"	$95	$90	Saucer	$30	$30
Bowl, 7-1/2" banana split, ftd.	$75	$65	Sherbet, low ftd.	$25	$22
Bowl, 8-1/4" celery	$40	$30	Sherbet, low flared edge	$30	$26
Bowl, 8-3/4" deep salad	$85	$70	Sherbet, tall ftd.	$50	$50
Bowl, 9-1/2" oval vegetable	$70	$65	Sugar w/lid, 3"	$120	$110
Candlestick, low, pr.	$50	$50	Sugar, 4-1/2" ftd.	$20	$20
Creamer, 3-1/4"	$30	$30	Sugar, rectangular	$20	$20
Creamer, 4-1/2" ftd. (amber $75)	$20	$20	Sugar, flat with cover	$200	$180
Creamer, rectangular	$20	$20	Sundae, ftd., ruffled top	$90	$70
Creamer & sugar on tray, 4"	$80	$75	Tray, center-handled	$195	$155
Cup	$60	$55	Tray, rectangular sugar & creamer	$80	$50
Goblet, 9 oz.	$80	$65	Tumbler, 8 oz., 4-3/16" flat	$120	$110
Ice bucket	$60	$53	Tumbler, 6 oz. ftd.	$40	$40
Marmalade, notched lid	$195	$160	Tumbler, 8 oz., 5-1/4" high, ftd.	$35	$30
Mustard, covered	$150	$125	Tumbler, 11 oz. ftd.	$60	$50
Parfait	$75	$70	Tumbler, 12 oz. ftd.	$70	$70
Pitcher, 64 oz.	$150	$160	Vase, 6-1/2" ruffled edge	$110	$90
Plate, 6-1/2" sherbet	$35	$35	Vase, 9-1/2" straight	$75	$70
Plate, 8-1/4", luncheon	$35	$30	Vase, 11" ruffled edge	$225	$275
Plate, 10-1/2", 2-handled	$50	$45	Vase, 11" straight	$140	$125
Relish, divided	$25	$20			

Imperial Glass Company, 1929
Colors: green, amber, pink,
blue, yellow

This swirl pattern was described as *Twisted Optic* by Imperial. The rolled console bowl, the candy dish, coasters, and candlesticks make this an interesting table ware pattern to collect.

The overall pattern design is identical to that of *Spiral* other than the base and the majority of the items in this pattern have a counterclockwise spiraling. The *Spiral* items are oriented in a clockwise direction.

Green 8" luncheon plate
illustrating pattern

TWISTED OPTIC

	Blue, Canary Yellow	All Other Colors		Blue, Canary Yellow	All Other Colors
Basket, 10", tall	$85	$40	Plate, 7" salad	$6	$4
Bowl, 4-3/4" cream soup	$17	$12	Plate, 7-1/2" x 9" oval with indent	$9	$5
Bowl, 5" cereal	$10	$6	Plate, 8" luncheon	$8	$4
Bowl, 7" salad	$15	$10	Plate, 10" sandwich	$15	$9
Bowl, 9"	$25	$15	Powder jar w/lid	$70	$40
Bowl, 10-1/2", console	$35	$20	Preserve		$30
Bowl, 11-1/2", 4-1/4" tall	$50	$25	Sandwich server	$40	$25
Candlesticks, 3" pr.	$40	$20	Sandwich server, two-handled	$18	$12
Candlesticks, 8" pr.	$60	$30	Saucer	$4	$2
Candy jar w/cover, flat	$55	$25	Sherbet	$10	$6
Candy jar w/cover	$60	$30	Sugar	$14	$7
Cologne bottle w/stopper	$65	$45	Tumbler, 4-1/2", 9 oz.		$6
Creamer	$15	$8	Tumbler, 5-1/4", 12 oz.		$8
Cup	$10	$4	Vase, 7-1/4"	$60	$25
Mayonnaise	$35	$20	Vase, 8", 2 handle, fan	$80	$35
Pitcher, 64 oz.		$30	Vase, 8", 2 handle, straight edge	$80	$30
Plate, 6" sherbet	$4	$3			

Vitrock

10" dinner plate

Oval platter, dinner plate, salad plate, cup, saucer

**Hocking Glass Company, 1934-37
Colors: white, fired-on colors**

Vitrock is both a dinnerware pattern and a kitchenware pattern. This was Hocking's plunge into the production of milk glass. A bit more expensive than Hazel Atlas's Platonite, it appealed more to those willing to spend a few extra cents. Its quality was far above Platonite. A raised flowered rim rises deeply above the very simple white blanks. Made to resemble embossed china, it sometimes was produced in fired on colors in solid red or green. Also to be found are decal-decorated centers.

VITROCK, "FLOWER RIM"

	White
Bowl, 4" berry	$5
Bowl, 5-1/2" cream soup	$18
Bowl, 6" fruit	$6
Bowl, 7-1/2" cereal	$7
Bowl, 9-1/2" vegetable	$18
Creamer, oval	$6
Cup	$4
Plate, 7-1/4" salad	$3
Plate, 8-3/4" luncheon	$5
Plate, 9" soup	$35
Plate, 10" dinner	$9
Platter, 11-1/2"	$35
Saucer	$3
Sugar	$6

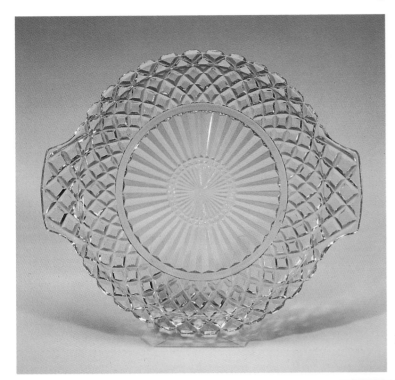

Anchor Hocking Corporation, 1938-44
Colors: pink, crystal, green, yellow, opaque white

There are some collectors who refer to this pattern as *Waffle*; however official company catalogs do list it as *Waterford*. By the time this pattern was released, Americans were somewhat weary of colored glass, thus its production as pink glass lasted only one year. In 1939, it was released in crystal with added pieces and it rose in popularity. But World War II cut its production short, with only a few occasional pieces offered in 1944.

Reproduction Note: In the 1950s, the old 13 ½" sandwich plate was modified and released as a five-section relish plate. Red and green inserts were produced. 5 ¼" crystal goblets were also reproduced.

Handled cake plate illustrating pattern

WATERFORD "WAFFLE"

	Crystal	Pink
Ash tray, 4"	$8	
Bowl, 4-3/4" berry	$7	$20
Bowl, 5-1/2" cereal	$18	$35
Bowl, 8-1/4" large berry	$10	$25
Butter dish and cover	$25	$230
Butter dish bottom	$7	$30
Butter dish top	$19	$200
Coaster, 4"	$4	
Creamer, oval	$5	$12
Creamer (Miss America style)	$35	
Cup	$7	$15
Cup (Miss America style)		$45
Goblets, 5-1/4", 5-5/8"	$16	
Goblet, 5-1/2" (Miss America style)	$40	$115
Lamp, 4" spherical base	$30	
Pitcher, 42 oz. tilted juice	$24	
Pitcher, 80 oz. tilted ice lip	$32	$160
Plate, 6" sherbet	$4	$8
Plate, 7-1/8" salad	$6	$10
Plate, 9-5/8" dinner	$12	$30
Plate, 10-1/4" handled cake	$10	$18
Plate, 13-3/4" sandwich	$10	$28
Relish, 13-3/4", 5-part	$16	
Salt and pepper, 2 types	$9	
Saucer	$3	$6
Sherbet, ftd.	$4	$15
Sherbet, ftd., scalloped base	$4	
Sugar	$5	$13
Sugar cover, oval	$5	$25
Sugar (Miss America style)	$45	
Tumbler, 3-1/2", 5 oz. juice (Miss America style)		$125
Tumbler, 4-7/8", 10 oz. ftd.	$15	$30

Handled cake plate, sugar bowl w/cover, creamer, butter dish w/cover

10 oz. tumbler, cup, 5 ½" cereal bowl

9" Dinner plate

Jeannette Glass Company, 1936-46
Colors: pink green, crystal, red, delphite

Some very remarkable pieces are available in *Windsor* including square relishes, a heavy, boat-shaped bowl, and pyramid candlesticks. Other interesting pieces include a powder jar and cover, a legged 7-inch bowl, and oblong trays.

Some of the first advertisements for this pattern included a picture of Windsor Castle in England for which this pattern was named. The pink color disappeared in 1940 with crystal pieces being made into 1946. As collectors amass a table set in pink, they quickly discover that many shades of pink were produced ranging from a pure pink to a peach pink tone.

The most difficult items to find are the pink candle holders.

Dinner plate, salad plate, sherbet plate, cup, saucer, footed sherbet

Above: Small berry bowl, 8 ½" berry bowl, 8" straight bowl, boat-shaped bowl
Below: Oval platter, open handled sandwich plate, cake plate

Above: Sugar bowl, creamer, salt and pepper shakers
Below: 52 oz. pitcher with four 4" water tumblers

WINDSOR

	Crystal	Pink	Green		Crystal	Pink	Green
Ash tray, 5-3/4"	$15	$45	$50	Plate, 7" salad	$5	$16	$25
Bowl, 4-3/4" berry	$5	$10	$12	Plate, 9" dinner	$6	$30	$30
Bowl, 5" pointed edge	$5	$25		Plate, 10" sandwich, closed handle			$25
Bowl, 5" cream soup	$8	$25	$30	Plate, 10-1/2" pointed edge	$10		
Bowl, 5-1/8", 5-3/8" cereal	$9	$24	$25	Plate, 10-1/4", sandwich open handle	$7	$18	$20
Bowl, 7-1/8", three legs	$8	$30		Plate, 13-5/8" chop	$12	$45	$45
Bowl, 8" pointed edge	$15	$60		Platter, 11-1/2" oval	$8	$20	$25
Bowl, 8", 2-handled	$7	$18	$25	Powder jar	$15	$60	
Bowl, 8-1/2" large berry	$7	$20	$22	Relish platter, 11-1/2" divided	$15	$240	
Bowl, 9-1/2" oval vegetable	$8	$22	$28	Salt and pepper, pr.	$20	$40	$55
Bowl, 10-1/2" salad	$15			Saucer	$3	$5	$6
Bowl, 10-1/2" pointed edge	$30	$140		Sherbet, ftd.	$4	$12	$15
Bowl, 12-1/2" fruit console	$28	$120		Sugar & cover	$12	$30	$35
Bowl, 7" x 11-3/4" boat shape	$20	$35	$40	Sugar & cover	$15	$130	
Butter dish (two styles)	$30	$55	$95	Tray, 4", square, w/handles	$5	$10	$12
Cake plate, 10-3/4" ftd.	$9	$20	$23	Tray, 4", square, wo/handles	$15	$60	
Candleholder, one hdld.	$15			Tray, 4-1/8" x 9" w/handles	$4	$10	$16
Candlesticks, 3" pr.	$25	$90		Tray, 4-1/8" x 9", wo/handles	$12	$60	
Candy jar and cover	$20			Tray, 8-1/2" x 9-3/4", w/handles	$7	$25	$35
Coaster, 3-1/4"	$4	$15	$20	Tray, 8-1/2" x 9-3/4", wo/handles	$15	$100	
Comport	$10			Tumbler, 3-1/4", 5 oz.	$10	$30	$40
Creamer	$5	$14	$15	Tumbler, 4", 9 oz. (red $55)	$10	$25	$35
Creamer	$8			Tumbler, 5", 12 oz.	$10	$35	$65
Cup	$4	$10	$13	Tumbler, 4-5/8", 11 oz.	$10		
Pitcher, 4-1/2", 16 oz.	$25	$125		Tumbler, 4" ftd.	$10		
Pitcher, 6-3/4", 52 oz.	$15	$30	$60	Tumbler, 5" ftd., 11 oz.	$15		
Plate, 6" sherbet	$3	$5	$8	Tumbler, 7-1/4" ftd.	$20		

Criss-Cross water pitcher ($35) and four tumblers ($10 each)

Paneled Optic pitcher ($65) with four handled mugs ($55 each)

Those Miscellaneous Pieces

While the preceding patterns are the more recognizable of the Depression era, there remain countless items which follow. While many of them do have specific pattern identification names, they are not produced in complete sets.

Many of them were meant to be marketed alone, and not with accompanying pieces. Some are candy dishes, some are wonderful candlesticks, some are utilitarian kitchen pieces, and some are just decorative in nature. Regardless, any of the following items would be magnificent additions to any collection.

Paneled Optic pitcher ($35) with two sizes of tumblers: juice ($8 each) and water ($8 each)

Footed floral goblets of heavy green glass ($20 each)

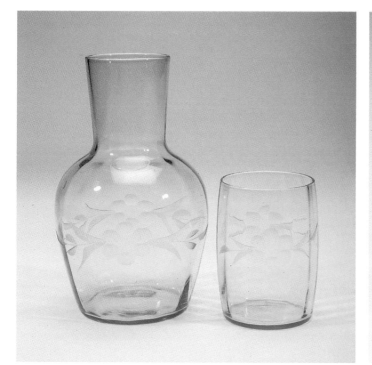

Night water bottle with water tumbler ($85 for set)

Cracked ice footed water tumblers ($110 each)

Etched sugar and creamer on tray ($50)

Dresser set of green glass in simple optic pattern ($120)

Green berry bowls ($6 each)

Pink quilted large berry bowl ($25) with individual berry bowls ($6 each)

Pink etched salad plate with ground glass bottom ($10 each)

Salt and pepper shakers in glass handled tray ($40)

Pink luncheon set in simple optic design: plates ($8 each), saucers ($3 each), cups ($5 each)

Console bowl in pink ($20)

Footed console bowl with simple etching ($35) and three-footed etched candy dish ($15)

Sparkling four-footed candy dish ($25)

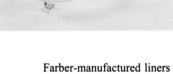

Farber-manufactured liners with divided candy dish glass inserts ($35 each)

Assortment of simple, yet elegant Depression candlestick holders ($10 to $15 each)

Bibliography

Anderton, Johanna Gast. *The Glass Rainbow.* North Kansas City, MO: Trojan Press, 1969.

Florence, Gene. *Collector's Encyclopedia of Depression Glass.* Paducah, KY: Collector Books, 1998.

Florence, Gene. *Pocket Guide to Depression Glass & More.* Paducah, KY: Collector Books, 1997.

Kovel, Ralph and Terry. *Kovel's Depression Glass & American Dinnerware Price List.* New York: Crown Trade Paperbacks, 1995.

Luckey, Carl F. and Marry Burris. *Depression Era Glassware.* Florence, AL: Books Americana, Inc., 1994.

Stout, Sandra McPhee. *Depression Glass in Color.* Des Moines, IA: Wallace-Homestead Book Co., 1970.

Stout, Sandra McPhee, *Depression Glass in Color Book Two.* Des Moines, IA: Wallace-Homestead Book Co, 1971.

Weatherman, Hazel Marie. *Colored Glassware of the Depression Era.* Springfield, MO: Weatherman Glassbooks, 1970.

Weatherman, Hazel Marie. *Colored Glassware of the Depression Era 2.* Springfield, MO: Weatherman Glassbooks, 1974.

Yeske, Doris. *Depression Glass: A Collector's Guide.* Atglen, PA: Schiffer Publishing, 1997.